Portrait of William Smith O'Brien

(from *The Felon's Track* by Michael Doneny.)

A NARRATIVE

OF

THE PROCEEDINGS

OF

THE CONFEDERATES OF '48,

from the suspension of the Habeas Corpus Act, to their final dispersion at Ballingarry.

THE REV. PHILIP FITZGERALD, D.D. & P.P.

BOOKS ULSTER

First published in 1868.

This new edition published in 2015 by Books Ulster. Text based on the first edition of 1868.

Typographical arrangement © Books Ulster.

ISBN 978-1-910375-25-9 (Paperback)

ISBN 978-1-910375-26-6 (Kindle)

Front cover illustration: *Attack on the Widow M'Cormack's House, on Boulagh Common, July 29th, 1848.*

PUBLISHER'S NOTE

A few minor changes have been made to the text of the original edition. For example, all instances of the place name 'Kilenaule' have been changed to *Killenaule* as both spellings were used in the narrative. Similarly, occurrences of 'Farrinrory' have been altered to *Farrenrory*. A small number of typographical errors have also been corrected. Father O'Carroll's MS was headed 'Chapter XII' and yet there were no preceding chapters X or XI. Accordingly, this has been changed to 'Chapter X'. The note references were in a state of confusion, but are *hopefully* now corrected to the way the author intended. The temptation to provide translations for Latin phrases was overcome on the basis that it is better to have no translations than bad ones.

CONTENTS

CONTENTS

A NARRATIVE OF THE PROCEEDINGS OF THE CONFEDERATES OF '48

As I have not yet seen a full and correct account of the memorable attempt at insurrection of '48, and its consequent outbreak at Ballingarry, and having been successful of late in procuring copious and well-authenticated materials for this purpose, I now intend to give, in an abridged form, a summary of the principal events which occurred from the 22nd to the 29th of July; that is, from the public declaration of resistance to the Government, by its leaders, to their final dispersion. The time is short, and yet within this brief period of seven days are crowded together many and various incidents which deserve to be remembered. The subject naturally divides itself into three parts. Of the first six days the narrative is derived from the Confederates themselves. Of the last day, on which all their grand schemes were frustrated and dissipated into thin air, my own account will be given as coming under my immediate observation; and the last part is taken from the diary of an unexceptionable witness—the late much-lamented and highly-esteemed Pastor of Clonoulty, the Rev. Thomas O'Carroll, who from their own dictation wrote down the statements of the chiefs of the Confederacy, and had them authenticated by their signs manual. If he had not been prevented by an unexpected and premature death, it was his intention to publish them, than whom none was more competent. His style was plain but attractive; simple but impressive; which imparts a charm to any subject of which he treats, *nihil tetigit quod non ornavit*. His death was the cause of grief to many, and to none more than the writer of these lines, who, through life, enjoyed his confidence and friendship, and to whom it now affords a melancholy consolation to cast a chaplet on his tomb.

For a long time past I intended to write this narrative, but two obstacles intervened. First, a want of materials, for, though I knew from report most of the facts, they were not sufficiently authenticated for publication. This difficulty has been removed by the kindness of the Rev. James O'Carroll in giving me the MS. of his deceased brother, whom he worthily represents and imitates in every virtue of head and heart. Secondly, it is not easy to write impartially of present subjects, whilst the chief actors are living, without giving offence. Of this the Roman poet warned his friend as *periculosæ opus plenum aleæ*. This obstacle also no longer exists. During the comparatively short period of twenty years most of them have disappeared—

> "Some sleep far off beyond the wave,
> And some in Ireland too."

After the abortive attempt to get their arms from the police, the leaders fled in different directions. S. O'Brien to the county of Kilkenny, and through Urlingford to

Thurles, where he was arrested;—some to Slievenamon and Waterford, and others towards the mountains of Kilnemanagh.

The last-mentioned were Thomas Francis Meagher, Leyne, Cantwell, and O'Donoghue, who, exhausted from fatigue and hunger, were hospitably entertained by the Rev. John Mackey, the venerated Parish Priest of Clonoulty, whose humanity made him forget for a moment the perils of the law and afford them more refuge than was consistent with his own safety.

The movement of '48, notwithstanding its abrupt termination and trivial results, will be always considered important from the station and character of its authors. Men of great daring and energy of mind, of courage and capacity to contrive great projects, but wanting prudence and foresight to put them in execution. Most of them were possessed of much talent and learning, and one in particular (whose tragic fate all deplore,) might have ranked with the first orators of the age, if he had made the study of eloquence a profession.

The MS. containing these materials is of undoubted authenticity, and will reveal facts which cannot fail to prove the more interesting, because they are but little known. Though written in the same hand, it is the joint production of all. It is, indeed, written with studied obscurity to prevent its being of use to the government, if by any accident it should fall into their hands. The sentences are alternately French and English, occasionally intermixed with Latin, with some words written in short hand. Besides, the leaders have Roman names, such as Lentulus, Decius, Demetrius, &c., which makes it difficult to be understood, and would be almost unintelligible, but that it is accompanied by a paraphrase of Father O'Carroll, in his own beautiful autograph, written under their immediate supervision, and submitted to their approval.

CHAPTER I

MS. OF CONFEDERATES

22nd July.—Dillon and Meagher left Dublin, on their way to Wexford, and arrived at Enniscorthy on Sunday, the 23rd, from whence they went to John Mahers, Esq., Ballinkeel, where they met S. O'Brien, and after having discussed the consequences likely to follow from the Suspension of the Habeas Corpus Act, they resolved on resistance. After breakfast, all three left for Enniscorthy,—where Meagher and Dillon, having heard Mass, they, with Smith O'Brien, addressed a vast concourse of people in the Main-street, who showed a disposition to engage in the approaching conflict.

At one o'clock they left for Kilkenny, and on arriving at Grague they visited General Cloney, where they were received with cordiality; vast numbers of the people here came to them, and received them with enthusiasm: the three addressed the multitude; on leaving, the people accompanied them a mile. They pursued their journey to Kilkenny, through Gowran, and having stopped here to visit the ruins of an old church, the people of the district expressed much sympathy with their cause.

They reached Kilkenny at nine o'clock: the city was very much excited. S. O'Brien addressed the people and clubs, and announced to them that probably in a few days they would be called on to defend their liberties. Retired to the house of Dr. Kane.

Monday, 24th July.—On this morning the presidents of clubs waited on S. O'Brien, Dillon, and Meagher at the same house. They agreed, in case of an attempt at arrest, that the city should be barricaded, and the people summoned to arms; in case of no such attempt, that the citizens should be held in a state of preparation for a recourse to extremities. It was found, however, on a more minute inspection that the clubs were badly armed.

At one o'clock they started for Carrick. At Callan, on their way, they were delighted with the indications of excitement and enthusiasm of the people. A vast multitude of the peasantry had assembled in the streets to receive them, and most of the houses in the town were decorated with evergreens. The triumvirate addressed the people, and called on them to rise against the Government. Several officers and men of the 8th hussars were present during their harangues.

Continuing their journey they stopped a short time at Nine-mile-house to take some refreshment, which consisted of oat-bread, milk, and eggs. During their stay here they got into conversation with some of the peasantry, who declared to them that they were prepared to rise.

They reached Carrick at nine o'clock in the evening. So soon as their arrival was announced the streets became densely thronged with people. Presidents and chiefs of clubs assembled at the house of —— with a view to communicate with S. O'Brien, who said he was prepared to begin, and, if he had 500 men, he would proceed to Cashel. They replied that they were not prepared, as they were totally taken by surprise, and that before engaging in such a struggle they should have more strength, and a more matured organization. They promised, however, to act.

S. O'Brien promised to proceed to Cashel, where Doheny had engaged, some time previously, to furnish 200 men in arms, on an emergency. Leaving directions that the people of Carrick should hold themselves in readiness to act at the first warning; and in case of Cashel being attacked, that Carrick should send 300 men, he left for Cashel. To this the presidents of clubs assented, and pledged themselves to use their utmost efforts to effect it. The whole night was spent in preparations.

Before starting, however, O'Brien and Meagher addressed the people, stating that the time for action had arrived; that they had avoided this last resource as long as any hope remained of gaining their liberties without an appeal to arms.

It was late in the evening when they left for Cashel. They reached Fethard at midnight, and after taking a hasty supper there, continued their journey, and at two o'clock, on the morning of Tuesday reached the city of the kings.

Leyne had been despatched to Newgate to consult Gavan Duffy and others with him about the course they were to pursue, who recommended them to proceed to the South and join O'Brien and Meagher. Accordingly, Leyne, Devin Reilly, and Halpin having met by appointment at Clonaskea Bridge, they started from Dublin, at half-past two o'clock, and having learned that O'Brien was at Enniscorthy, directed their route thither; reached there that night and went to bed. At Ballinkeel they heard that S. O'Brien had left for Kilkenny, whither they followed by car, through Borris and Gowran, and arrived there at half-past six, where a cattle show was being held. They started for Cashel, through Urlingford, where they arrived at half-past five.

CHAPTER II.

THEIR ARRIVAL IN CASHEL

Tuesday, 25th July, the triumvirate reached Cashel, as was said before, at two o'clock, on the morning of Tuesday, and went directly to Doheney's, who was not at home. There they were told that P. J. Smith and Cantwell were at Littleton's, whither they went, and having called them out of bed to hold a council of war, it was resolved that the barrack should be attacked, and the soldiers disarmed. To this Littleton and his sons were opposed. They raised objections on account of the absence of Doheny and other causes. The members of clubs also, when consulted, refused their co-operation with one exception.

P. J. Smith* is sent to Thurles, and thence to Dublin, to instruct the clubs to tear up the railways at five different points, beginning at Thurles. Meagher is sent to Carrick to lead forward the men of Ballybricken to occupy Carrick, and proceed to Nine-mile-house, where it was arranged that he should meet Smith O'Brien, and there concentrate their strength. John Littleton was ordered to accompany Meagher with a commission to Doheny to bring the mountaineers from Slievenamon, and was instructed to proceed afterwards to Clonmel to advise the clubs to keep the Queen's forces in check. Meantime the elder Littleton ordered the parties to quit his house, oth-

---

* See Note 1, page 103.

erwise he would be compelled to report their treasonable practices to the authorities. All left and went to Doheny's. O'Ryan is sent on a mission to Clonmel. He left at three in the morning, and was back at seven. A message was also conveyed to Clonoulty, to Dr. O'Mahony, who had promised to join the party at fifteen minutes' notice, but did not come at all, and said he always believed there was no real intention of fighting. O'Brien and Dillon retired to rest, Cantwell keeping watch.

It was now plain that everything threatened a total failure in Cashel. Had they succeeded in taking the barrack, it was intended to unfurl the green banner from the rock, and to issue a proclamation,* announcing the formation of a Provisional Government, and the declaration of an Irish Republic; but under their present circumstances it was considered necessary to depart forthwith from the city. After a short consultation with his friends, O'Brien resolved to try Callan and its neighbourhood, and with this view they started for Killenaule on two cars. S. O'Brien, Dillon, and O'Donoghue on the first car, and Stephens and Cantwell on the second.†

At Killenaule, O'Brien addressed the people in presence of the police, who gave expressions of sympathy and approbation; and on several parts of the road to Mullinahone he harangued large assemblages of men who came out to meet him.

---

* See note 2, page 103 and note 7, page 108.
† See note 3, page 104.

CHAPTER III.

THEIR ARRIVAL AT MULLINAHONE

At four o'clock they arrived in Mullinahone. Here also a great concourse of people had assembled in the town, and received them with the greatest enthusiasm. O'Brien waited on the Rev. Mr. Cahill, who argued the impropriety and imprudence of such a course, principally on the plea of its being premature. The people continued to assemble from Modeshaland other places. Towards night there were at least 2,000 men armed with guns, pikes, and pitchforks. O'Brien, Cantwell, and Wright continued to drill them during the night till three o'clock next morning. The chapel bell tolled.

Wednesday, 26th July, O'Brien, O'Donoghue, and Stephens proceeded at seven o'clock, a.m., to the woods, in the neighbourhood of the town, accompanied by a large body of people. Mr. C. gave permission to cut down trees for the purpose of barricades, and marked with an X such as he thought best fitted for that object. Having given directions for the erection of the barricades, and impressed on the people the necessity of retarding the progress of the Queen's troops, Mr. O'Brien, accompanied by O'Donoghue and Stephens, entered the police barrack about eight o'clock, and forthwith summoned the constable and five men stationed there to surrender. Two of the police were engaged in preparing breakfast, and others were in the act of shaving. All were taken completely by surprise, and manifested unequivocal symptoms of alarm. To Mr. O'Brien's summons to surrender, the sergeant replied that such a course would be ruinous to them and their families, and that they would never do so unless Mr. O'Brien marched up to their door with a hostile force of 30 or 40 armed men. Some of them declared that if their honour were thus saved they also were prepared to join the movement. Mr. O'Brien, touched by the sergeant's appeal, and the avowed sympathy of his men with the cause, said that he did not wish for any unnecessary effusion of blood, that he would give them half an hour to deliberate, but that, in case they persevered in offering resistance after that time, he would burn them out of their barrack. After half an hour he returned, but found on entering that the entire party had privately marched off in the direction of Callan.

At nine o'clock, Messrs. O'Brien, O'Donoghue, Dillon, and Cantwell breakfasted in the house of Mr. Wright, a Protestant gentleman—who had received his education in Trinity College,—with his mother, sister, and a younger brother, who had all embraced the popular cause. After breakfast Mr. Corcoran, the parish priest, waited on Mr. O'Brien, and warmly expostulated with him on the imprudence of his attempt before the harvest, and urged on him, ere he had yet compromised his cause, to postpone it till that period. To which Mr. O'Brien replied, with some warmth, that if Mr. Corcoran so wished, he would surrender himself at that moment into his hands. Mr. C. begged of the gentleman not to mis-understand him, and, that so far from recommending such a course, he was entirely indisposed to cause his arrest, or co-operate in it. After which Mr. C. and his friends departed.

Just as these gentlemen retired, two fine young fellows from Ballingarry presented themselves in arms, and requested to be introduced to S. O'Brien. They represented to him that there were already 500 men in arms at Ballingarry, who held themselves in readiness to act according to his directions. Before giving any order on the matter Mr. O'Brien thought it of importance to obtain some accurate information regarding the movements of Mr. Meagher, and with this view he despatched O'Donoghue and Cantwell to Carrick.

CHAPTER IV.

MR. MEAGHER GOES TO CARRICK AND WATERFORD TO BRING REINFORCEMENTS

After having parted with his friends at Cashel, on the night of Tuesday, the 25th, Meagher proceeded towards Kiltinan, at the foot of Slievenamon, for the purpose of obtaining an interview with Doheny, who, he heard, was concealed in the fastnesses of that mountain with a small party of about 20 men, and urging on him the necessity of bringing all the forces he could collect to the assistance of O'Brien at Cashel. Having heard from some mountaineers that Doheny had left an hour before for Carrick, Mr. M. continued his journey in that direction, and, in the neigbourhood of Carrick, and about two miles outside the town, met his friend Mr. O'Mahony, at a forge, superintending the manufacture of pikes. This forge being near his (O'M.'s) residence, Mr. M. dismissed his car and went with O'Mahony to his house, where he met Doheny, who had only a little before arrived there. After taking a sleep of about two hours Mr. M. proceeded along the Suir opposite to Coolnamuck, on his way to Waterford, and, at nine o'clock in the morning, crossed the ford on horseback, accompanied by O'Mahony and a guide.

Having passed the river at Coolnamuck, he found a covered car for Carrick, which had been ordered by O'M 's servant, waiting to receive him. Here, having parted with his friends, he continued his journey through Portlaw to Waterford. When passing through Carrickbeg, one of the wheel-bands of the vehicle broke; this accident occasioned considerable delay. Whilst being repaired Mr. M. retired into a house on the roadside, where he heard that pikes were making through the whole country round, and that the people were in readiness, as soon as called on to co-operate. He reached Waterford about four o'clock, p.m., and privately made his way to the residence of the Rev. Mr. F., and there learned that the city was in a state of great excitement, and that there were five war steamers in the river to keep the people in check.

Whilst here, a report reached the city that Cashel was taken by Smith O'Brien, and that the military and police had surrendered their arms. On hearing this, Mr. Meagher immediately after dinner, wrote a letter to the secretary of the Wolfe Tone Club, directing him to arm the members of that club, and to hold them in readiness to march at half-past ten o'clock that night, each man having been previously provided with provisions for three days. He pointed out the old Cork road, as the line of their march, and engaged to meet them at twelve o'clock, near the village of Portlaw.

Having at eight o'clock, sent a letter conveying these instructions to Mr. Condon, the Secretary, Mr. Meagher procured a car from the city, and went on direct to

Portlaw. Dismissing the car within two miles of that village, he withdrew into a grove where, overpowered by fatigue and loss of rest he fell asleep, and did not awake for more than two hours. On awaking he found it was midnight, and consequently that the hour had arrived when his friends should be approaching. He listened—he endeavoured to catch the sound of the measured tread of men advancing in military array; but no such sound fell on his ear—all around was the silence and solitude of the grave. Burning with impatience he retraced his steps towards Waterford, but had not proceeded more than half-a-mile when he was met by three men, of whom Condon was one, who said that his letter did not reach him 'till nearly two hours after its being dispatched and that it was literally impossible for him at that advanced hour of the night to collect men and equip them for the journey; Mr. M. bitterly regretted the disappointment, as he had engaged to meet Mr. O'Brien at Callan, on the following day, at the head of the men of Ballybricken, but as the performance of this engagement was now impracticable, and as it was necessary to apprise Mr. O'Brien of the cause of the disappointment, it was agreed that Mr. M. should start for Callan to meet O'Brien—Condon having engaged to furnish 600 men, well armed and provisioned, with the greatest expedition, on receiving a letter from Mr. M. to that effect. After this, the parties separated. Mr. Condon and one of his companions returned to Waterford, Mr. M. and the other proceeded to Carrick, which they reached after a rainy and inclement night, at four o'clock in the morning, (Wednesday, 26.)

When approaching the bridge of Carrickbeg, Mr. M. and his companions were met by two labourers, who told them they could not pass the bridge, as it was defended by twenty policemen with bayonets fixed, and loaded carbines. One of the poor men invited the weary travellers into his humble dwelling, which was convenient—an invitation which was very thankfully accepted. Here oaten bread and whiskey—the only species of refreshment the house afforded were placed before them, and whilst they were feasting on them, five or six of the neighbours came in and entered freely into conversation with the strangers on the subject of the approaching troubles. Here Mr. M. learned for the first time that it was the general opinion that the movement was premature—that the people were without food, and that the enemy would destroy the crop before it could be gathered in, and thereby take away all means of subsisting the patriot army during a protracted struggle; meantime the woman of the house having learned the quality of her visitor, and the wretched state to which he was reduced by rain and fatigue, said "Sure it would drive us to anything to see you a born gentleman, cast from the lap of luxury upon the world in this way, and if Father Byrne would only give us the word, it is little we'd think of ourselves." During this conversation a covered car arrived from the town, in which Mr. M. and his companion immediately drove off to O'Mahony's, and there went to rest, as on the morning before, and slept for three hours.

Here Mr. M. was met by Rev. Mr. Byrne, who begged of him not to begin the movement so soon, as the country was not prepared for it, and implored of him in the most passionate terms to flee to America and wait for a more proper time. Above all, he besought him not to make Carrick the theatre of the outbreak. To these expostulations Meagher replied that it was quite out of the question, his going to America; that were he to do so, he would thereby forfeit the confidence of the people, and that Gavan Duffy and John Martin would be transported before his return; which would so damage their cause as no subsequent efforts could repair. He promised, however, to communicate with O'Brien and to exert his influence with him, that the first operations should not take place at Carrick, though it was expected that Carrick would act at the commencement of the rising. Father Byrne said he did not object to have Carrick act as an auxiliary, but that he was decidedly opposed to have it made the head-quarters. Towards the close of the interview, Meagher said that he felt convinced that they would be compelled to fight within eight days at most; to which Father Byrne replied that even that time, short as it was, would be of great advantage, as it would give the people an opportunity of being better prepared. Mr. Byrne returned to Carrick and Meagher sat down to breakfast.

Just, however, as he was preparing to start for Callan, to join O'Brien, Messrs. Leyne and Halpin arrived with the intelligence that all O'Brien's movements were unproductive of any beneficial results—that there appeared to be no concert among the leaders, nor enthusiasm among the people—that Devin Reilly had left Cashel and proceeded in quest of Doheny to Slievenamon, where both were at present hiding amongst the ravines and caverns of the mountain.*

After a long conversation in O'Mahony's garden, it was at last resolved that Halpin should start that night for Dublin, with positive orders to have the railway torn up at five or six different places, so as to prevent the troops from being concentrated at Thurles and Kilkenny, and with instructions to the Dublin clubs to be ready for action, in case of any movement in the city.

Meagher and O'Mahony had not proceeded far in the direction of Callan, when a messenger overtook them to say that a party of dragoons from Carrick was in full pursuit of them, for the purpose of arresting Meagher. On hearing this, both the gentlemen leaped from the car, and immediately fled towards Slievenamon. Meagher flung his green military cap into a ditch, and after a long run reached Mr. Coghlan's farm-house at two o'clock, where he went to bed for a few hours.

Meanwhile, Leyne and Halpin stopped for dinner at O'Mahony's, and, after an interview with Mandeville, a

---

* Messrs. Leyne and Halpin, having parted with Devin Reilly at Cashel, who henceforward united his fortune with Doheny, and took refuge with him in the fastnesses of Slievenamon, directed their course to Carrick, in quest of M., where a Mr. Kavanagh, learning their object, conducted them through the narrow lanes of the town to the house of O'Mahony, where they found Meagher preparing to start for Callan.

confederate, it was agreed that Leyne should join Meagher, and remain with him till such time as O'Mahony and Mandeville could be able to raise the peasantry in their district, whilst Halpin should start direct on his mission to Dublin, as already determined.

Towards evening Leyne, accompanied by his friend Halpin, was conducted to Coghlan's farmhouse, where Mr. M. was staying. Here the friends parted. Leyne slept with Meagher, and henceforward became his companion in all his perils and sufferings; whilst Halpin, instead of fulfilling his engagement, immediately on his arrival in town went to the rooms of the League, and there coolly penned and published an inflammatory letter, for which he was arrested the following day. Halpin travelled in the disguise of a priest.

At twelve o'clock on Wednesday, 26th July, Mr. O'Brien despatched from Mullinahone Cantwell and O'Donoghue, with a letter to Meagher: they had just gone half way, when they were met by Dr. O'Ryan, conveying a letter from Meagher to O'Brien. After a short consultation it was arranged that both parties should exchange letters and return back. When Cantwell and O'Donoghue had reached Mullinahone, they learned that Mr. O'Brien had left for Ballingarry, at the head of a large party. They followed and overtook them within two miles of that village, accompanied by a multitude of people, wild in their enthusiasm, because their parish priest, the Rev. E. Prendergast, drove at their head, and, as it were, by his presence consecrated their cause. (See note 5, page 106)

CHAPTER V.

ARRIVAL AT BALLINGARRY, AND SPEECHES OF O'BRIEN, DILLON, &c.

This enthusiasm was, however, suddenly damped, and in a quarter where it might have been expected that an effort would be made to turn it to good account in favour of the movement. For Mr. O'Brien had no sooner reached Balhngarry than he addressed the people from the chapel wall. He spoke of the struggle in which they were about to engage, and asked his hearers would they allow him to be arrested by the Queen's troops? They, of course, declared with one voice that they never would. He next told them that as their cause was a holy one, it should not be disgraced by any outrage on person or property, and that he would punish with death any one of his followers who would injure the property of any man—that he would now dismiss them all for the night, retaining only twenty men to form a bodyguard, and that he expected that every man whom he then addressed would return to his standard at an early hour the next day, supplied with provisions for at least four days; the quality of provisions which he would recommend was oatmeal bread and hard eggs.

Mr. Dillon next addressed the meeting, but at once perceived that his words found no response in the hearts of his hearers, nor was he altogether unprepared for such a result, when he recollected that most of those he was then addressing, were prompted to join the movement solely in the hope of being fed. Indeed to any one it must have appeared little less than solemn mockery of their wants, to tell a people living on a daily allowance of a pound of Indian meal to return on the following day bringing with them, every man, four days' provisions. The people dispersed downcast and dispirited, and from this day forward never again came together in such numbers.

At seven o'clock Messrs. O'Brien, Dillon, O'Donohue, and Cantwell sat down to dinner, and were shortly after joined by Doheny and Devin Reilly, from Callan. During dinner the conversation naturally turned on the course they were to pursue, in order to insure success. Dillon thought it an act of fatuity to engage in such a movement, and utterly impossible to prolong it for any time without resorting to the usual expedient of making the property of the country support those who were battling for the interests and independence of the country. Besides, with regard to Ireland, there was a more imperative reason to demand the adoption of this course. The property of the nation was, in a great measure in the hands of the national enemy, and would unquestionably be employed against us. Convert this property for the present to national purposes and you thereby secure means for subsisting your army, and deprive the foreign enemy of one of his most potent auxiliaries. Doheny was for taking Carrick, and seizing on the bank of that and other towns, which he would make subserve the national exigencies. All present dissented from this opinion as injurious to the people, and calculated to bring disgrace on their cause. But Mr. O'Brien went farther, and declared that under no circumstances whatever would he be induced to assent to the line of policy pointed out by Mr. Dillon, for reasons repeatedly expressed by him already. Devin Reilly could see no prospect of the ultimate triumph of their cause from the agencies at present available. They had none of the elements of success, and he recommended that the struggle be postponed for three weeks, when the nation would be in a better position to resist; the harvest would be gathered in—Father K—— would be ready with a large force to act by that time, and he, Devin Reilly, had the strongest assurance from Major L., that he had 10,000 men in the County Tipperary and other places under drill, which he would be able to bring into the field at the same period. O'Brien was totally opposed to any farther delay, and would not consent to have the struggle postponed for a single day, on which Doheney and Reilly retired to Slievenamon.

After dinner barriers were erected on the roads leading to Templemore and Callan, and twelve men, armed with guns and pikes, were stationed to defend each. At eleven Mr. O'Brien inspected the barricades previously to his retiring to rest. Messrs. Dillon, O'Donohue, and Stephens also stretched themselves on a pallet for a few hours, Cantwell having remained up to inspect the guards on the barricades.

Before O'Brien retired to rest, two deputies arrived from Kilkenny to inform him that the garrison of that city was reinforced since the previous Monday, and that of the seven hundred men enrolled in the clubs there, only fifty were returned as armed and ready to co-operate. After making their report the deputies got back to Kilkenny, under favor of the night, without having encountered any danger on the way.

About one o'clock, O'Brien was called up by two countrymen, armed with pikes, who presented themselves before him, with a gentleman whom they had made prisoner at some distance from the village, and whom they believed to be a spy. This gentleman was no other than Terence Bellew MacManus, an ardent confederate, who had come direct from Liverpool, on hearing that the people had appeared in arms. He was, however, the herald of discouraging news. He stated that he had endeavoured to procure two hundred armed men from the Liverpool Clubs to undertake a secret expedition, where he was certain of success, and yet the clubs could not furnish that small number out of their united body; his contemplated enterprise consequently failed. He purposed to surprise a depot of arms and ammunition, badly defended in the vicinity of Liverpool, and after making himself master of these munitions of war, to sail immediately with his whole force to Wexford, where he hoped to raise and arm the peasantry in his progress through the country. He had three small steamers chartered at Liverpool, to transport his men thither with the least possible delay.

MS. OF CONFEDERATES

At two o'clock, on Thursday, 27th, O'Brien, Mac-Manus, and Stephens took charge of the barricades, thereby giving Cantwell the advantage of a few hours' sleep, previous to his being employed on a more active and perilous mission during the day. At three o'clock O'Mahony arrived with a letter from Meagher to O'Brien, requesting him to fall back on Slievenamon with all his force, which course, O'Brien thinking to be the best in the critical circumstances in which he was placed, was resolved to adopt, and with this view retained O'Mahony till a late hour in the afternoon, expecting the people would come in considerable numbers to join him during the day. But he had the mortification to witness the fatal effect which his speech of the previous evening had on the minds of the people, for they did not come in any considerable numbers.

CHAPTER VI.

DEPUTATION TO TEMPLEDERRY

At five o'clock Cantwell was despatched with a letter for Father K. exhorting him to take the field at the head of his men, and thereby create a diversion in his neighbourhood. As this mission was of an urgent nature, Cantwell seized a farmer's horse and rode to Littleton, from which place he continued his journey by the mail car to the suburbs of Thurles, having first committed the horse to the care of a man who engaged to have him returned to his owner. At Littleton he was joined by G. B., who succeeded in procuring at Thurles a private car, which conveyed them to Templederry, without encountering the suspicions of the police.

On presenting their letter, Mr. K. declared he could not think of acting on its suggestions, as he totally condemned the course pursued by O'Brien, as fatal to the cause. He recommended them, however, to see Mr. Dowling, of Newport, who was ready to act on hearing from Mr. O'Brien. It was then agreed that Butler should return to Mr. O'B., whilst Cantwell would go in quest of Dowling, and see what might be done through his agency in furtherance of the movement. On reaching Newport he found that Dowling had just gone in the direction of Keeper-hill to avoid arrest, as he had learned that six detectives were on his track for several days before. Cantwell pursued him thither, and at seven in the evening found him in a respectable farmer's house at the foot of the mountain, ready to take to the hills at the first signal of pursuit. The two started for Templederry towards night-fall, and after a toilsome and arduous journey over the hills, and through unfrequented glens, they reached their destination at one o'clock the next morning. On calling at a farmer's house in the neighbourhood, to seek shelter for the night, they were surprised to find there Messrs. Meagher and Leyne, who had arrived about an hour before.

We have seen already that O'Mahony was despatched by Meagher, at a late hour on Wednesday night, with a letter to O'Brien, suggesting the necessity of his falling back on Slievenamon, and that he was not permitted by O'Brien to return with an answer till a late hour on Thursday evening, though he had engaged to Meagher to be back before sunrise on that morning. Weary of expectation, and impatient of further delay, Meagher, accompanied by his friend Leyne, started at two o'clock in the evening from Slievenamon for Templederry, where they arrived at midnight, and finding Mr. K. to be from home, put up for the night at a farmer's house in the neighbourhood. When passing through Borrisoleigh they had occasion to call on a friend, and during the few moments they remained in conversation with him, their car-driver was accosted by the police, who wished to know the names and business of the travellers. The driver with much promptitude and presence of mind replied, that they were students from the College of

Thurles, going home for vacation. The readiness of the car-driver's reply disarmed all suspicion, and the two travellers, favoured by the dusk, passed through the town without being recognised or exposed to further scrutiny, though the streets were literally thronged with police and detectives.

At seven o'clock the next morning Mr. K. invited the four gentlemen to his house to breakfast. Here he reiterated his condemnation of the course pursued by O'Brien, and could foresee nothing but disaster and defeat to result from it. "See, gentlemen," said he, "it is purely utopian to attempt revolutionizing a country, or expect to conduct it to any successful issue, through the agencies employed by O'Brien. If you are in earnest you must engage the very passions of the people, nay, you must work on their worst passions, and make them subserve the movement. You should seize on all the property of the country—the corn, the cattle, nay, the very plate of the enemy should be secured and converted into cash for the payment of foreign officers, who will hereby discipline your army. You should seize on the person of every aristocrat, and every other friend of the government, and hold them as hostages; and should the enemy, brutal as he probably would be, so forget the usages of legitimate warfare, as to shoot all the prisoners taken by them, on the plea of their being rebels, you will have it in your power to retaliate, by executing one of their friends and allies for every man of yours so treated by them." Such is an outline of the views entertained by Father K—— on the subject of revolutionary war. These views he discussed in detail, and with such force of argument, as to impress his visitors with a high opinion of his capacity to organize and direct the movement, if he could be induced to embark heart and soul in the struggle. This, however, he declined to do, and so the deputies departed, at eight o'clock, to join O'B. once more at Slievenamon.

Just as they were about to start, word was conveyed to them that I. F. Lalor, a prominent confederate, was arrested during the night at a house in the neighbourhood. This intelligence warned them of the necessity of hastening their depature from the place; and so, after having directed their course through the mountain roads, they overtook O'B. at three o'clock in the evening, a few miles beyond Killenaule, on his way to the commons of Ballingarry.

We shall now return to Mr. O'Brien, and the other leaders, whom he left at Ballingarry, on the morning of Thursday, the 27th, engaged in defending that village against any sudden approach of the enemy.

At five o'clock on that morning Cantwell was despatched on his mission to Templederry, and with what result we have already seen.

CHAPTER VII.

THE PROCEEDINGS AT BALLINGARRY

At seven Mr. MacManus was ordered out to reconnoitre the country, and, if possible, to bring some accurate intelligence regarding the movements of the police and troops. To effect this object he volunteered to ride into Callan, and, with this view, seized on a horse of Mr. Going's, of Ballyphilip. At different parts of the road he exhorted the people to join the national banner, and endeavoured to inspire them with the same degree of enthusiasm for the cause which burned in his own patriot breast. About 600 of the peasantry were collected during the forenoon, of whom 50 were armed with muskets, and about 150 with scythes, pitchforks, and pikes. Mr. O'B. reviewed and exercised the men armed with muskets, in street and hedge-firing for better than an hour, and Mr. Dillon drilled the pike-men during the same time, principally instructing them in the mode of making a charge, and performing some other simple evolutions. Stephens was employed to direct the manœuvres, and frequently afterwards expressed his astonishment at the dexterity with which these humble peasants used their weapons, and their surprising aptitude in learning and performing these military exercises.

During the day MacManus returned from Callan, and reported a large military and constabulary force stationed there, and under orders to hold themselves in readiness to march into the disturbed district.

Shortly after a messenger arrived to say that a gentleman resided about four miles distant who had fifty stand of arms in his house. Stephens and MacManus were ordered with twelve musketeers by Mr. O'Brien, to go and capture them, and in case of resistance, to attack the house. The party departed on their mission, but had scarcely gone a mile and a-half when a courier, despatched by O'Brien, countermanded them, and ordered them back. On their return they found all the people drawn up in line, and immediately an order was given to march towards Slievenamon. The fifty musketeers, commanded by Dillon formed the van, the pikemen, led by O'B. closed the rere, whilst the baggage and unarmed portion of the people moved along in the centre.

CHAPTER VIII.

SECOND VISIT TO MULLINAHONE

At three o'clock, p.m., they arrived at Mullinahone, where they were received with the greatest enthusiasm, and an assurance that pikes were manufactured in great numbers since the last visit. Mr. O'B. here, at his own expense, supplied every man with a two-penny loaf and a cup of water. Towards the close of the refection the Rev. Mr. Cahill, the Curate of the parish, having recognised some of his people in the ranks, called a few of them aside and cautioned them of the terrible consequences that were sure to befall them unless they speedily abandoned their folly and returned to their homes, A great many went away, about 100 remained, and with these O'B. continued his march in the direction of Slievenamon. They had, however, proceeded scarcely a mile beyond Mullinahone, when nearly eighty of the number deliberately filed off, leaving only about twenty after them. In the presence of such a defection, and with such a wretched force, O'B., abandoned all idea of proceeding further towards Slievenamon. So dismissing the few followers that still adhered to him, he called his friends together and took their opinions as to what was most advisable to be done under the present discouraging aspect of their affairs. It was proposed that they should separate, every one into a different district, and organise the people—that he should throw himself upon his tenantry at Cahermoyle, and there form the nucleus of a more combined and general movement, with which local leaders would be able to co-operate, or if not, endeavour to gain the military and police of the district. After various projects were discussed and rejected, it was finally determined that another effort should be made in the neighbourhood around Slievenamon, which, from its natural position and its proximity to Kilkenny, Carrick, Waterford, Clonmel, and other seats of Confederate sentiment was so well suited for their purpose.

In this state of things rumour reached that the Callan police were preparing to attack them, when O'Brien gave orders to march towards Killenaule, and for this purpose got cars from Mullinahone.

The party started late in the evening, and arrived in Killenaule at half past one o'clock on Friday morning. On their way they met Mr. Butler returning from Templederry, who communicated to them all that had occurred.

In Killenaule they found the hotel guarded by five or six workmen, through fear of an outbreak. O'Brien asked what were the feelings of the people, and these men told him that they were all armed, and ready for action in his cause. After this he retired to rest.

CHAPTER IX.

IN KILLENAULE AGAIN

At seven o'clock on Friday, O'Brien ordered MacManus and Stephens to reconnoitre and report on the general aspect of the country. This order was no sooner given than countermanded by another to O'Donohoe and Stephens, that they would lead an armed procession through the town; which they did, accompanied by great numbers— from two to three hundred men. S. O'Brien ascended the neighbouring heights to take a survey of the surrounding country, and, whilst thus occupied, was told that a troop of horse were on their way to the town—this was a company of the 8th Hussars on their way to escort the Judge of assizes to Nenagh—and in a few moments the advanced guard rode up. At once, O'Donoghue, Mac-Manus, (called out of bed,) Dillon, and Stephens went to erect barricades in the main street—carts, ladders, beams of timber, and creels of turf were quickly brought together, and in twenty minutes three large barricades were erected. MacManus goes up the hills from which O'Brien had just returned. He (O'B.) was compelled by the others to place himself in the rere of a house near the first barricade, with a view to his safety. At this moment a general shout announced the approach of two troops of horse, on which Dillon mounted the first barricade, with stones in both his hands. Stephens did the same, armed with a rifle, and presented it at the officer in command.

A labouring man also, to whom S. O'Brien gave a rifle, and twelve or fourteen of the inhabitants, armed with pikes and guns, defended the barricades. The officer requested leave to pass, and asked if there were any more barricades in his way. O'Donoghue replied there were two others well defended, and desired Dillon to parley with the officer in command till O'Brien's wishes were known as to what course they should pursue. His orders were to allow the officer to pass, if he would pledge his honour that he would not arrest S. O'Brien. The officer having done so was allowed to pass amidst cheers from the people.

CHAPTER X.

THEY RETURN ON FRIDAY EVENING TO THE COMMONS OF BALLINGARRY

At eleven o'clock O'Brien, Dillon, O'Donoghue, Mac-Manus, and Stephens proceeded by car to the collieries. O'Brien harangued the people on different occasions along the road. At the cross of Glangoole, on the way to New Birmingham, he erected barricades to obstruct pursuit, and about half a mile farther on he took shelter from the rain. He was shortly after joined by Mr. Byrne and others. Meagher and Leyne, with those who were sent to consult with Father K——, having heard that O'Brien was at Killenaule hastened thither to meet him; but on their arrival were told he had left two hours before for the collieries. They followed, and about three o'clock overtook him on his way to the commons. Here all the leaders were collected together—the greatest number that had met for a considerable time, viz., O'Brien, Dillon, O'Donoghue, Doheney, Leyne, Meagher, Cantwell, MacManus, Devin Reilly, Stephens, and O'Mahony, with many others. All proceeded to the commons, accompanied by a great multitude. A council of war was immediately held to deliberate on the course they ought to pursue. O'Brien was unanimously voted to the chair. The different members succesively expressed their opinions.

O'Brien refused to say anything, lest his address might influence others in expressing their opinions. Dillon recommended to take a house in Kilkenny, and from it to issue a proclamation announcing an Irish republic. Devin Reilly declared he would sooner be shot than witness another like this day's exhibition—boys and girls, and unarmed men, neither capable of offering resistance, nor of affording protection. With one voice, indeed, all condemned such a mode of warfare as fatal to success. O'Brien remained inflexible, though all were unanimous that the best thing to be done was to take different directions—every one in his own district to raise the peasantry, create diversions, and thereby distract the enemy. Dillon, however, continued with O'Brien, more from a sense of honour than the hope of effecting any good, or a desire to be considered as approving of his mad project. He was ultimately persuaded by Meagher to leave for Roscommon, and try if Athlone could be taken. Even O'Brien consented to this as the only way of escape remaining for him. He also begged of the rest, nay, commanded them to leave him and consult for their own safety, to which at last they reluctantly yielded. Meagher, Leyne, O'Donoghue, and O'Mahony went towards Carrick, through Ballingarry, and stopped that night near Nine-mile-house. At Ballingarry they met a body of men, preceded by fife and drum, going to join S. O'Brien at the commons. Leyne made them a present of a green flag. Devin Reilly and Doheny returned to their old haunts on Slievenamon, and were not seen afterwards. Of all the rest only MacManus and Stephens remained with Smith O'Brien.

Saturday, 29.—Leyne, Meagher, and O'Donoghue remained till night on Mockler's-rock, near Carrick, waiting the return of a courier they had sent to Ballingarry, who misled them by a false report of O'Brien's proceedings there on that day. They, however, remained this night, and the following day (Sunday), at ——, higher up on Slievenamon. At night they were joined by O'Mahony and MacManus, who came from the commons, and also by P. J. Barry, and Gray of Dublin. The two last having come unexpected, were to them objects of suspicion, and accordingly they devised a plan to get rid of them. They were ordered off on a mission to Dublin, but were seen in Carrick on the following day, and, to excuse themselves, pretended it was Meagher and Leyne who ought to have gone. Leyne, Meagher, O'Donoghue, and MacManus retraced their steps, and having been conducted over hills, were kindly received by —— at Peafield, where there were three brothers, who acted nobly towards them. On Monday, (the 31st,) they remained concealed in heather the entire day. At length, on a car being ordered from Fethard, they drove through Holycross to Clonoulty, and, at four o'clock on Tuesday, knocked up T. Molony out of bed. Leyne started on the mid-day train for Limerick, with important despatches from Meagher to Mr. K., his solicitor; and letters from MacManus to MacC. Having arrived in Limerick, at a quarter past two o'clock, he was exposed to much danger from policemen and detectives, and had to wait two hours at Morris's hotel before he saw those he expected. Left by the half-past five o'clock train for Tipperary, then started by car for Clonoulty, and reached Molony's at half-past ten o'clock. Here scouts gave notice of alarm, at which the party fled to the fields, but reassured, they returned, remained an hour, and then slept in T. K.'s barn.

Wednesday, 2nd Aug.—Went through Glenough, and slept at a peasant's hut; but wishing to avoid Holycross we had a narrow escape from policemen.

4th Aug.—All day in the fields; slept at Father Denis's, but were turned out by James.

End of the MS. of the Confederates.

Here I will take the liberty of mentioning an anecdote of Father Denis, so characteristic of his good nature, that I hope to be excused for introducing it. Through life he was distinguished for hospitality, and on the occasion of seeing fine young fellows outlawed and exiled for loving Ireland, "not wisely, but too well," his inmost soul yearned with sympathy for them. He gave them food and entertainment, and with other necessaries, he also supplied them with linen, of which they were much in need. By doing so, he never thought he was transgressing any law, human or divine, until some friend reminded him, that he had been an accomplice in treason, and subjected himself to its severest penalties, which so terrified him, that for the first time in his life he regretted having been hospitable.

MY OWN ACCOUNT

INTRODUCTION

The following narrative of events, which occurred in this neighbourhood in the summer of '48, has been suggested by different versions of them which have gone abroad; some giving me too much credit, and others too little, and mostly all founded on erroneous impressions. From this brief record of them it will be seen, that my part in them was not the result of choice, but of necessity; and that I had no wish to be the adherent of either party, but a mediator between both. If by it, error be removed, and matters appear in their true light, the only object I have in view will be accomplished. To vindicate my own conduct and motives from misrepresentation, and the people from much obloquy, I thought fit to notice, in a general manner, the previous current of events, which led to so abrupt and unexpected a termination.

This narrative does not pretend to elegance of style or diction. It is chiefly a circumstantial history of facts; which will be more easily excused in a person whose life is one of labour, not of study, and whose business is more in the cabins of the poor, than in the saloons of fashion or the abodes of the rich.

I can hardly expect that it will not displease many, as it treats both parties with equal impartiality. But to praise or censure I am alike indifferent, as I only wish to give a truthful account of what I witnessed.

MY OWN ACCOUNT

It is the only—perhaps the best legacy—I can leave to a people whom I esteem and love, that it may serve, on one hand, as a warning against slavish subserviency to those in power, who abuse their authority for selfish purposes, who traffic on the administration of the laws, who banish justice from her legitimate tribunal, and render the commission of the peace odious or contemptible; and, on the other hand, to inculcate rational obedience to constituted authorities, to dissuade them from secret societies and every illegal combination, and especially, that they may be never again deluded into any crude and abortive and foolish attempt at rebellion.

P. FITZGERALD.

BALLINGARRY,
March 1, 1868.

PERSONAL RECOLLECTIONS

—"thy chains as they rankle, thy blood as it runs,
But make thee more painfully dear to thy sons,
Whose hearts like the young of the desert bird's nest,
Drink love in each life-drop that flows from thy breast."

Moore.

Often reflecting on the outbreak of the Insurrection in this parish in the summer of 1848, I always believed that so long expected an event was connected with very few circumstances worthy of being commemorated, and that, if the brief history of the last week of July in this year were consigned for ever to oblivion, the loss to posterity would be inconsiderable. For, whether it is to be attributed to the depressed condition of the population produced by the unexampled sufferings of a famine of three years' continuance, or to the incapacity of its authors, or to the efforts of government to frustrate their measures by anticipating them, it is certain that no failure could he more signal; nor does the memory of man easily furnish another instance of preparations made with so much persevering endurance, and threats of so much violence, terminating in equal disappointment. Too much occupied with the labours of the mission, and meditating only on fulfilling its duties, I had neither leisure nor inclination for other pursuits, nor any intention of taking farther notice of this subject, which has for years been numbered amongst the things that were; but the solicitation of others, whose judgment I respect more than my own, has induced me to adopt a different course, and to give a simple narrative of the circumstances which occurred in this parish and neighbourhood, of which I was an eye-witness, and reluctantly compelled, whether for good or ill, in its last and closing scene to have a considerable share.

"Quæque ipse miserrima vidi et quorum pars magna fui."

If I should fall into any mistake, it will not be from favour or partiality, as I never had any connection with either party, being alike indifferent to both, and equally disapproving of their policy. For I thought that, if the government were as anxious to prevent the famine as to put down rebellion, the difficulty would not be greater in one case than in the other; and yet the people were left to die in thousands and tens of thousands, without any legal enactment for their relief, when the suspension of the Habeas Corpus Act was only the work of twenty-four hours' legislation. And on the other hand, I considered that to resort to violence was the worst possible way of redressing grievances, and that the achievement of a nation's liberty would be too dearly purchased by the effusion of human blood.

From the passing of the Relief Bill to the Repeal Agitation, the country seemed to enjoy a state of uninterrupted tranquillity, as if the people regarded this long-sought boon as the accomplishment of all their wishes.*

---

* For some years after, till the settlement of the Tithe Question, the kingdom was much disturbed by the opposition everywhere given

But when, after some year's experience, it was found that the same hostile spirit which resisted it so long, still frustrated the law and deprived it of any salutary effect, a widespread feeling of indignation began to burn in the hearts of the people, which required only a breath to be rekindled into a flame. When O'Connell trusted too confidingly to his alliance with the Whigs, and saw his forbearance rewarded with their habitual perfidy, he had no other resource but in an appeal to the country. His reappearance on the popular arena was hailed with shouts of enthusiastic delight. The word "Repeal," as himself used to say, had a magic sound with the people, and no other went more home to their hearts. The voice which before from the Corn Exchange roused the nation from its lethargy, and shook by its thunder the portals of the constitution, was listened to by thousands with renewed rapture. The peasantry, who travelled from a distance of many miles, hung upon his accents with mute astonishment, and would be ready to scale the rampart

---

to its collection, people believing it a very great grievance to have to contribute to the support of two churches, one of which they loved as much as they hated the other. But this resistance was not insurrectionary; it was not against the government, but against an obnoxious statute, and was only passive, unless when its payment was enforced by the aid of military and police.

This desultory warfare against an odious and tyrannical impost was attended in many places with the loss of human life and the effusion of much blood, until its final settlement in 1836, when it was converted into rent-charge; the name only being changed, and the abomination itself continued.

or face the cannon's mouth at his command. History affords no other instance of a whole nation so subdued to the will of one man, who possessed no authority over them but that which was acquired by the majestic power of his eloquence, and their unbounded confidence in his moral honesty and sincere devotion to their cause. What Napoleon was to the army, O'Connell was to the people—their idol. The State Trials gave the first shock to this peaceful organization, as well as to the mighty mind by which it was moved and animated. He outlived his imprisonment a few years, but he never recovered from its effects. The Repeal flag was again unfurled, and monster meetings held; but this was a final and transient effort. Of the gigantic energy of mind and body, which no labour could exhaust, which defied delay, and confronted, unappalled, the greatest perils, a wreck only remained. But what the State Trials began, the Secession and the Famine accomplished. Sinking under the weight of age and declining health, he felt unequal to the conflict, and as a suitable close of a life devoted to the service of religion and country, he proposed to visit the Tombs of the Apostles, a blessing which he did not live to enjoy,—and closed his eyes in a strange land, far away from the country of his affections and the people he so dearly loved.

The attainment of civil and religious liberty by means prescribed by law, was the doctrine always proclaimed by O'Connell, whether he designed it to be general and applicable to all cases, or adapted only to the constitution under which we live; but to me it would appear certain, that, in any sense or interpretation of it, and however qualified it may be, he never intended practically to deviate from it. The Young Ireland Party powerfully co-operated with him in the great agitation for Repeal, but always inculcated, in poetry and prose, a different doctrine, viz., that to resort to arms was sometimes just and necessary, when other means were ineffectual—a doctrine also maintained by the leaders of the Rebellion in '98, and sanctioned at the Revolution by the conduct of those who, to guard against unconstitutional aggression, placed a foreign prince upon the throne, and expelled the legitimate and reigning monarch. This doctrine, though often avowed, did not receive its full development till 1846, when its advocates seceded from the Association, and formed a distinct and separate body. After the secession, its advisers openly promulgated their purpose of making an appeal to arms, which they vindicated by referring to the calamitous state of the country.

They held that allegiance and protection were reciprocal, and should co-exist or cease together; and that, if ever resistance was lawful, it was when the kingdom was desolated by famine; when the people were dying in multitudes; when strong men fainted in the streets from hunger, and mothers with infants at their breasts, were lying dead upon the highways; when cemeteries were red with new-made graves, and, in many places, from the immense mortality, the dead were cast in heaps into the same pit, unshrouded and coffinless. This case, which was not at all exaggerated, seemed plausible enough, and might in the opinion of many, afford a sufficient cause, if, before its final adoption, they had better considered their means of carrying it into execution.

The people were accordingly made to listen to language, to which for thirty years previous they had been unaccustomed. Before, they were warned not to transgress the law, or go beyond the boundary marked out by the constitution; now, they are advised to set law and constitution at defiance. Before, it was often repeated to them, that the greatest advantages would be too dearly purchased by the shedding of one drop of blood; now, they are told it is only in the battle-field that any advantage can be obtained. Heretofore, they were told that passive obedience, and to act only in self-defence, were the means of asserting their rights, which are now to be sought for in the din of arms and tumult of war. It is unnecessary to say, that such appeals, often repeated in a forcible and impassioned style of eloquence, to a people steeped to the lips in misery and destitution, and by men who proved themselves at least trustworthy and sincere by their self-devotion and the sacrifices they were prepared to make, as well as the great perils to which they were exposed, were heard with attention, and produced a powerful effect.

Accordingly, in the beginning of '48, the excitement was very great, and increased daily, till the danger became imminent. Every moment the outbreak was expected, though no one could pronounce how soon it would occur; but especially in the month of May, when the trial of John Mitchel took place, under the new bill of treason-felony. No one thought that the apostle and proto-martyr of physical force would be allowed to leave the country for a penal settlement, without a practical illustration of his doctrine. However, it passed away with great threatening and excitement, but no hand was raised to prevent his removal. A feeling of indignation spread throughout the kingdom, which gave the enemy a temporary triumph, and was considered a proof of weakness or pusillanimity for having lost a great opportunity. Many expressed surprise and regret that Ireland should be deprived of so illustrious a patriot when she most required his aid. But the crisis had not yet arrived. It was only accelerated by this event, as well as by the seizure of the *Tribune*, *Felon*, and *Nation* newspapers, which quickly followed.

These repeated aggressions of the government, though they failed to provoke hostilities, were answered in the usually strong language of menace and defiance. Many thought that the insurgents were only biding their time—waiting till their plans would be more fully matured, and that their rising would be more sudden and powerful; while others regarded it more as a symptom of weakness than of prudence and foresight. To me it is very clear that both parties looked forward to the time of harvest, but with very different views; one, eager to anticipate it, and the other anxiously expecting it; for it was easy to foresee that suddenly raised forces, undisciplined and disorganized, could not by any probability be kept together in the present scarcity of provisions. Whether the rebellion would prove more formidable in September than in July, may admit of doubt; but it is certain, that by anticipating the season of plenty, the government disconcerted all their plans. But that which precipitated hostilities, and rendered a conflict inevitable, was the suspension of the Habeas Corpus Act, and the offer of a large reward, with a warrant for the arrest of Smith O'Brien.

Forewarned by the fate of John Mitchel, and the effect of the atrocious system of jury packing, he resolved not to be its next victim. From Wexford, where its announcement first reached him, he proceeded to the city of Kilkenny, visited St. Canice's Cathedral, and, from the summit of the Round Tower and Cromwell's Chair, took a view of the surrounding country.

CHAPTER I.

S. O'BRIEN IN CALLAN

On Monday, 24th July, he arrived in Callan, which is six miles east of Ballingarry. The news of his arrival there produced the greatest excitement throughout the neighbourhood. The shock of an earthquake, or the eruption of a volcano, could not have caused greater alarm. To this many circumstances contributed. His character, which was deservedly high; his station in society; his connexion with the aristocracy, especially those who were most distinguished for their opposition to popular rights, and their attachment to the government against which he was now in arms. He himself started on Tory principles, was returned to parliament as such in the commencement of his public career, but, endowed with a strong mind and generous nature, he was soon able to extricate himself from the trammels of family influence. His greatest enemy will admit, that it was his sympathy with the abject state of misery to which he saw the country reduced by misrule, that made him by degrees a convert to liberal opinions, and ultimately placed him in the foremost ranks of the people.

It has been said that the pride of a noble and illustrious lineage had some influence on him; concerning which, I can offer no opinion. But I know that his family is amongst the most ancient in Europe. It was old when Greece and Rome were in their infancy. Before the foundations were laid of the Parthenon and Acropolis, its kings swayed the sceptre of Ireland; and many generations of its dynasty had passed away, when Evander occupied the Palatine Mount, and before the she-wolf suckled the twin-brothers, one of whom founded the Seven-Hilled City, and bequeathed to it an immortal name.

Sunday, the 23rd of July, was a day of much trepidation and anxiety. The rumour spread everywhere that Smith O'Brien was amongst them, outlawed and proscribed; that with a chivalrous and daring spirit he had thrown himself upon the country, and volunteered to be their leader; that he had done all that could be expected from him, and performed his own part; and that it remained only for the people to do theirs—to place themselves under his banner, and to supply him with men and the munitions of war; that such an opportunity may never again be presented to them of delivering themselves and all that they held dear from the iron yoke of their oppressors; and that it was better and more honourable to meet death bravely fighting with arms in their hands, than to endure a slow and lingering death by famine in the bosom of their families.

Never indeed did any appeal receive a readier and more willing response. Multitudes volunteered to rally round his standard. On the following Tuesday, hundreds went, and thousands would have followed, if the progress of events had accorded with their expectations. But never were the hopes of the people more sadly disappointed.

Those who went to meet him to Mullinahone, remained the whole day in the streets without food or shelter, some bread was distributed to them at his own expense, and they were told that in future they would have to procure provisions for themselves, as he had no means of doing so, and did not mean to offer violence to any one's person or property.

This announcement gave a death-blow to the entire movement. Those poor fellows returned home late in the evening faint with hunger, resolved not to expose themselves a second time to the same privations, who communicated this disheartening intelligence to others, which cooled the ardour that at first animated them, and made them regard the whole business as a wild and visionary scheme.

CHAPTER II.

IN BALLINGARRY

On Wednesday, perceiving that his followers had not increased, he came on to Ballingarry, attended indeed by a considerable multitude, but consisting chiefly of women and children, and not having in the entire procession more than fifty men capable of carrying arms. On the way, or at the village, he was joined by some of the leaders, who addressed the people from the wall in front of the chapel. On this occasion of the first visit to Ballingarry, there was not much done. The chief things were, a view taken of the hills above the chapel, to see if they would be favourable for encampment or to hazard a battle, some manœuvres for recruits, to accustom them to military exercises, and a few nominated to commissions in the army which was about to be raised.

On Thursday the village was crowded with an immense multitude of every age and sex. An irregular and confused mass assembled, many of them scarcely knowing the cause, as if they came there only to increase the number. Some ascended the belfry of the chapel, and kept ringing the bell all night, which for its novelty contributed to increase the alarm, and make the people think that something of moment was to occur on the following day.

It may seem strange that in any part of the kingdom the peasantry could be so ignorant of the storm which constantly threatened them for the last three years; and yet such was the case in this peculiar district, about twelve miles distant from the nearest market town, where the people were too much occupied with farming business and the collieries, to have much time to devote to political subjects, in which they took less interest than others. Some who read newspapers or visited the neighbouring towns, had an idea of the distracted state of the country; but the great body of the people seldom thought of it, and least of all did they imagine that the commencement of the outbreak would be amongst themselves.

Many went up and down, seeking information. "Was the movement good or bad? to be recommended or avoided? Who was Smith O'Brien? was he honest or otherwise? a friend or an enemy? perhaps a spy [some said] sent by the government, as was often the case before, to inveigle them into plots and conspiracies against it, and then to betray them?"

For these interrogatories I had no answer, for I had resolved to take no part with either side, having the same dislike to both; to the government, for letting the people starve, and to the popular leaders, for resorting to violent means to obtain redress. Though seldom unwilling to communicate any information I may possess, on this occasion I intended to act otherwise, and to be as reserved as possible. I believed Smith O'Brien to be honest and high-minded, and as far removed from fraud or dissimulation as any man living, and who, as was seen soon after, would expend his last farthing, and lay down his life, to secure the freedom and prosperity of Ireland; but I was determined not to make known my own impressions, to allow things to take their course, and if they wanted information concerning his character, to permit them to seek for it elsewhere than from me. Wishing to have no part in it, I never left the house during the week, unless when the duties of the mission rendered it necessary.

On Thursday I had to attend a sick person. I had only emerged from the avenue gate, when I found myself in front of a procession headed by a man whom I did not then know, but afterwards heard was Terence Bellew MacManus. Before we came near to one another he saluted me respectfully, being told, I suppose, by those around him, who I was, which, of course I returned with equal civility. Having approached nearer, he asked if I would join them. To which I replied in the negative, and stated my reason for refusing, to which he mildly answered: "Perhaps, sir, your way may be the best; but we have been driven to it, and it was our last resource." Here we parted; and with this exception, I never met any of the leaders again, till we met for the first and last time, on the following Saturday, on the heights of Farrenrory.

CHAPTER III.

S. O'B. GOES TO MULLINAHONE AND THENCE TO KILLENAULE

About eleven o'clock on Thursday the body left Ballingarry by the road to Killenaule; but when they came as far as the crossway which leads in opposite directions towards Urlingford and Mullinahone, they stopped for a short time, as if deliberating which road to take. At length they took the latter direction, and after their arrival there had to encounter the renewed, and if possible more vigorous opposition than on the occasion of their first visit. Both parish priest and curate exerted themselves to the utmost against them, and by remonstrance, argument, and entreaty, endeavoured to dissuade the people from following them. They expostulated with Mr. O'Brien and his immediate companions, and implored of them to desist from so frantic an attempt; that resistance to the government was useless; that they had no resources at their command, neither men, or money, or supplies of any kind; that the country would not second their efforts, and that they would only bring sure destruction and ruin on themselves and others.

Though this reasoning had not sufficient weight to induce them to retrace their steps, they did not consider it prudent to remain long in the neighbourhood of so much adverse influence; and, accordingly, they left on the following day for Killenaule with more favourable auspices. Here the aspect of things was entirely changed. The reception of Mr. O'Brien was most enthusiastic; bouquets fell in showers upon him, and addresses were read for him; but that there was any improvement in the way of order or organization, or any effective addition to his strength, I did not hear.

One incident worthy of remark occurred during his stay amongst them. Great alarm was caused by the appearance of a body of cavalry. All believed that the enemy was at hand, and prepared for battle. Barricades were thrown across the street, and means of resistance adopted. Smith O'Brien was not present. But one of the leaders who had mounted the first barricade with James Stephens, met the officer who commanded the party, which happened to be the 8th Hussars, and asked him if he had been sent to arrest Smith O'Brien; but when the officer replied that he did not even know that Smith O'Brien was there, and had nothing to say to him, but was on his way from Clonmel to Nenagh, he was allowed to pass unmolested.

CHAPTER IV.

THE COMMONS

In a circuitous course around the parish, it would seem as if their eyes rested constantly on the Collieries, as the place, of all others, most likely to afford them important aid. They knew them to contain a numerous and poor population, and many athletic fellows of much recklessness and daring, and who, from their dissipated and improvident habits of life, were likely to join in any attempt to subvert the Government of the country, as they had nothing to lose in any case, whatever might be the result. On Friday, therefore, they took leave of Killenaule, and, coming through Mardyke and Earlshill, arrived in the evening at the Commons, The Commons would seem, indeed, to have been previously selected for a general meeting; for, at the same time with Smith O'Brien, there arrived there also the principal members of the Confederation, viz., Michael Doheny, Thomas Francis Meagher, John B. Dillon, Devin Reilly, MacManus, O'Donoghue, James Stephens, John O'Mahony, Cantwell, Kavanagh, and others. Messrs. Meagher, O'Brien, and Dillon harangued the people, and explained their views in coming amongst them to solicit their co-operation. The manager of the Collieries was sent for by Mr. O'Brien, and commanded to deliver a letter from him to the Board of the Mining Company of Ireland—a letter which did him serious injury afterwards on his trial, and weighed so heavily in evidence against him. In all his other acts there was nothing to inculpate him directly of a design against the state—nothing that might not have been interpreted as undertaken in self-defence; but this fixed on the entire movement the character of a revolution, and tended more than anything else to convict him of the crime of high treason.

A council was held in a neighbouring house, in which the circumstances of their position, and the resources at their command, were considered, and the feasibility of their plans discussed. I cannot pretend to give with any authority a report of what occurred at this meeting, which was private; but the version of it that went abroad, and which from the result seems probable enough, was, that all, with the exception of Smith O'Brien, looked upon the whole business as lost irretrievably: that they had no sufficient means of resistance at hand; and that it was better to abandon the attempt, though late, than proceed to hostilities with such inadequate resources. Here some contention arose between the head of the Confederation and its members, which reflects equal honour on both. All were of opinion that the insurrection was at an end—that any farther attempt at resistance was impossible, and that all their aspirations for liberty and self-government were menaced with impending ruin. Despair was visible in every countenance, yet they were not dismayed, and were resolved unanimously to remain with him to the last—to be participators in his misfortunes as they were the associates of his ambition and of his hopes. This he steadfastly refused, as no good could come from it. His advice was that every one would consult for his own safety—that they would take different directions, and endeavour to rouse the peasantry, each in his own district, wherever they went, and, if they should hear that himself had raised the standard elsewhere, under more favorable auspices, that they would rally round him again. To this they could not assent. He begged, entreated, and expostulated, but in vain; and it was only when he commanded them emphatically that they yielded. All left with the exception of Stephens and MacManus, who alone remained with him.

That some may have expected to be able to raise auxiliary forces in other places, and to return in time with sufficient aid, is not improbable, and it was reported so at that time; but if such views were ever seriously entertained, it was only to be disappointed. Indeed, the history of the world does not afford a clearer illustration of the uncertainty of human foresight and the vanity of human events. For the last three years of incessant agitation, the kingdom was kept in a state of unprecedented excitement. Men of much talent and energy of mind, exerted all the powers of poetry and eloquence to produce this effect. All the arguments of reason and imagination were made use of to excite the people. Their tenderest sympathies were appealed to; their devoted attachment to religion and the homes of their forefathers, their patriotism and sense of injuries, which were pourtrayed in the sublimest verse and expressed in a style of glowing and impassioned oratory; the ruthless persecution of the landlords, and heartrending effects of extermination, were remembered, and the long continued famine studiously neglected, to reduce the number of the population to a less formidable standard.

The outrages of bygone days were not forgotten; the massacre of Mullaghmast, and the slaughter of Drogheda and Wexford, and of course, from the long account of the crimes of England against Ireland, the perfidious violation of a most solemn treaty, could not be omitted. They were reminded of the achievements of their ancestors at Benburb and Clontarf, and of the many records of Irish valour exhibited by their countrymen on the Continent, at Mantua and Cremona, and many a Confederate wished with the poet,

"That God would grant, and then he'd die with joy,
   One day on his own green land like that at Fontenoy."

By these appeals often and continually repeated, popular enthusiasm was raised to the highest pitch, so that all expected, and many burned with the desire of seeing the rival races committed to deadly conflict; Celt and Saxon confronted in battle array; and that at length a simultaneous and final effort would be made by the nation to cast for ever from her neck the heavy and galling yoke of long-continued oppression. The issue, however doubtful, it was believed would be sanguinary, and that victory, to whatever side it belonged, would be dearly won. But these grand ideas of the approaching struggle proved to be no more than the baseless fabric of a vision, or like the fine-spun labours of the spider, which, though the work of great toil and perseverance, may be blown asunder by a breath.

CHAPTER V.

ATTACK ON THE POLICE

On Saturday, the 29th of July, a day which was to see the termination of this long expected and much apprehended outbreak of popular feeling, Smith O'Brien found himself almost alone at the Commons, with only two or three of his devoted adherents, and about one hundred colliers, who remained faithful to him to the last, and were ready to defend his life at the sacrifice of their own. There seemed to have been no more cause of expecting an attack on this day than on any of the past days of the week; unless that, as the Government, which from the beginning had been so terrified, seemed now to be considerably reassured, from the slow progress of the insurrection, it was not likely to delay to strike the first blow. To one looking back, after a lapse of many years, to the relative state of parties so disproportioned in discipline and numbers, and so unequally prepared for hostilities, such great fear would seem almost incredible, if there were not the strongest proofs to convince us of it. All the Irish regiments were sent out of the kingdom, and English and Scotch introduced in their place. Batteries were constructed outside large towns. Barracks, even those of the police, were loopholed and surmounted with parapets to command a view of the enemy, Martello towers constructed along the coast to guard against invasion, and the constabulary in most places ordered into the neighbouring towns, which more than other things made the people believe that a perfect panic had seized the government, and that they regarded the rebellion as already formidable.

This impression could exist no longer. The slow progress made by Mr. O'Brien during the past few days had effectually dispelled it. It was, therefore, pretty clear that the enemy would take advantage of his feeble state, and endeavour to crush the infant Hercules in his cradle. Accordingly, the constabulary of Thurles, Kilkenny, Cashel, Callan, and Killenaule, received orders to leave at an early hour of the day, that they might reach the Commons at a certain time. The Callan police, however, whether by accident or design, left a long time before the others, and were in the village of Ballingarry, on their way to the Commons, where they would have arrived about eleven o'clock, if they proceeded direct to the end of their journey. News of their approach was conveyed to Mr. O'Brien, by a messenger who came a shorter way than the police, and had left Callan about the same time, but had outrun them considerably. There was, of course, much confusion caused by this intelligence amongst a mixed multitude of men, women, and children, in which the latter classes largely preponderated. About fifty men had fire-arms, and perhaps as many more had pikes and other rude weapons, with which the coal pits supplied them. To resist an attack of this kind, they wanted everything but resolution, of which indeed they seemed to have a sufficient share. A barricade was at once thrown across the road, to obstruct the police, behind which they were to take their stand, to prevent them from coming farther. But this precaution proved unnecessary; when at a distance of about half a mile, the police saw a vast multitude, which they considered to be all armed men, they turned suddenly to the right, and proceeded in all haste up the hill, by the road leading to the Widow Cormick's house, which they must have had previously in view, as it could not be seen from where they were, nor from any part of the road from Ballingarry to the Commons. On seeing this, the multitude went across the fields to meet them, and travelled so fast that both parties arrived at the house almost at the same time. The police had only just time to enter and close the door, when their pursuers were outside. So little time was there to spare, that the sub-inspector left his gray charger outside the wicket, with his pistols in the holsters of the saddle, to become the property of the first occupant. Mrs. Cormick had never suspected that this affair would at any time have given her any concern. She was gone about half way to the Commons, when a messenger followed her to say that her house was occupied by a strong party of police; and that all her children, five or six in number, of whom the eldest was no more than ten years, were shut up with them. She returned in a state bordering on frenzy, and having been introduced to Smith O'Brien, addressed him in no very polite language. "Was he the gentleman from whom the police had been compelled to take refuge in *her* house, and convert it into a barrack?

What was to become of herself and her orphans, should it be wrecked or destroyed? or where would she find a home? Herself was shut out from her children, and they were prisoners within. Could he not find some way of protecting herself and her little ones, and rescue them from the danger to which their lives were exposed?" This appeal, which might move the most obdurate, could not fail deeply to affect a man whose ear was never deaf to the voice of humanity. With great peril to himself, he came with her to the parlour window, and both were in conversation with the police, when some person from the crowd, probably under the influence of liquor, flung a stone against the kitchen window, when the police suddenly, as if only waiting for an opportunity, discharged from all parts of the house a volley of musketry upon a large and defenceless multitude, by which two men were killed, and many severely wounded. The people were at once dispersed, and hid themselves wherever they found shelter. Some took refuge under the arch of a limekiln, in front of the house, whilst the greater part retired to the road beneath, where, by the deep fences which covered the way on both sides, as well as their distance away from the house they were safe from danger. The police kept up a constant fire upon them as long as their ammunition lasted. It was here that I had the honour of seeing Smith O'Brien for the first and last time, having never seen him before or since.

From the time the firing began until our arrival, I could not speak of what occurred at the house, as an eye-witness; but from the narrative of those who had just come down, and having since so often heard it from many who were present, there cannot be any doubt concerning its veracity.

At the first volley, Mr. O'Brien withdrew from the parlour window, and passed through a wicket at the south end, which opened into a small cabbage-garden. Here he could have no protection from the constant fire kept up from the upper and lower stories, unless from a low wall, about four feet high. He had to creep along this until he reached some houses in the rere, around which he had to make his way to the road, where he met the multitudes who had descended from the front or eastern side. To any one who ever saw the place, his escape must appear exceedingly difficult, for, whilst sheltered only by the wall, and after emerging from the houses in the rere, he was wholly unprotected and exposed to the fire of the police.

With about a dozen of men, more determined than the rest, who refused to leave the house, was Mac-Manus, who indeed throughout the whole day showed more courage and resolution than any one else. With a musket in his hand, and in the face of the enemy, he reconnoitered the place and observed every accessible approach to the house, and with a few colliers, under cover of a cart-load of hay, which they pushed on before them, came up to the postern-door of the kitchen. Here with his own hand he fired several pistol-shots, to make it ignite, but from the state of the weather, which was damp and heavy, and from the constant downpour of rain on the previous day, this attempt proved quite unsuccesful. With men so expert at the use of the pickaxe, and so large a supply of blasting powder at the collieries, he could have quickly undermined the house or blown it up; but the circumstance of so many children being shut in with the police, and the certainty that, if they persevered, all would be involved in the same ruin, compelled him and his associates to desist from their purpose.

An incident, though trivial, which occurred at the village a few days before, may serve to give a better idea of his character. The servant of a neighbouring magistrate, who had gone with his master to Callan, was met by MacManus on his return, and asked if he would oblige him with a loan of his horse for some time. The servant, of course, demurred, but was compelled to comply, on which MacManus mounted, rode the horse for the day, and sent him to his owner in the evening with his compliments. With a few others of his daring, things would very probably have proceeded much farther, nor would the crisis have terminated so abruptly.

During the following week, troops poured in constantly. Encampments were made in different places, at Ballingarry, Killenaule, Turtulla, etc. As no lives were lost on the side of the government, martial law was not openly proclaimed, but the magistrates and those who had the command of the army, acted as if they possessed unlimited power. They held councils, ordered arrests every day, until the gaols were filled to suffocation, and threatened to shoot persons for walking quietly in the streets, or standing at their own doors. Prisoners were sent in shoals to Dublin, and detained there a long time; and though there were no executions, whole families were left mourning and desolate, for many died in captivity and exile, others perished from long concealment in bogs and mountains: some found a grave beyond the waters of the wide Atlantic, where not a few have achieved honourable distinctions and obtained there a hospitable refuge and a home.

CHAPTER VI.

MANY SENT TO NEWGATE

After their removal to Dublin, great fears were entertained that some of them would become informers; but these fears proved to be groundless. Their fidelity was severely tested. Menaces, and bribes, and promises of pardon were made use of, but without effect. Many of them were men of unblemished character, never before accused of any crime, and even innocent of any part in the insurrection. Of these no one entertained any doubt. But there were a few of a different class, in whom neither their fellow-prisoners nor any one else had much reliance; but these, too, were firm. One had been frequently convicted of theft; yet he was as true as the best amongst them. All said that he must have renounced his former vices, and undergone a complete and entire reformation of life, which, however, was not verified by subsequent events; for, soon after his liberation, he resumed his former occupation, though much disabled by a bullet wound received in the shoulder at Farrenrory. At the next assizes he was convicted of sheep-stealing, and sentenced to transportation, but died in Spike Island from the effects of his wound. With him this manner of life had been almost a profession. During the famine, as well as before it, he never felt much ashamed of it; but to be branded with the name of an informer, was a degree of degradation to which nothing could induce him to submit.

PERSONAL RECOLLECTIONS

Here the reader will excuse a short and simple narrative of my part in this transaction, which I was compelled to undertake, much against my will, having previously resolved to have nothing to do with it, and wishing as much as possible to avoid all connexion with it, which, indeed, would have been so if it had not occurred on this particular day of the week—a day in which it is necessary to be engaged in the chapel for many hours.

CHAPTER VII.

MY OWN PART IN THE PROCEEDINGS

About ten o'clock, a.m., I saw the Callan police passing through the village, on their way to the Commons, followed by a great crowd, some from curiosity, and many from motives of greater interest. The Rev. Patrick Maher (the late much-lamented curate of the parish) was with me, and I proposed to him whether it would not be better if we followed after them; that, perhaps, we might be able to do some good, or prevent some evil; or that, at least, our ministry might be necessary; in which view of the matter he readily concurred. We accordingly followed in sight of the police; but when they turned off from the direct road, we stopped back, and remained in conversation with some persons who stood about us. Whilst waiting here, a horseman rode up hastily, and suddenly halted on seeing us: he turned out to be Head-Constable Carroll, in coloured clothes, sent from Kilkenny by the stipendiary magistrate, to countermand the imprudent haste of the Callan police, and to prevent them falling in with the insurgents till the arrival of reinforcements from other quarters. It was just at this moment the firing began, and as soon as we heard the shots, we rode all three in full gallop until we arrived under Mrs. Cormick's house. Here we first met Mr. O'Brien and the party who had just retreated from the house. All were indignant that the police had fired on the people without provocation, and were anxious to go up again to the house. I was asked if I would go with them, and when I refused, Mr. O'Brien asked what would I advise them to do, and said that he would act as I would recommend; an answer which I did not expect, as I often heard that he was rather self-willed, and determined to follow whatever himself considered best. I was never more perplexed. I saw that if they returned to the house, the police would very probably be all killed, for I believed that any resistance on their part would be worse than useless; and, as a consequence, that martial law would be proclaimed throughout the kingdom, and the atrocities of '98 again renewed.

Mr. O'Brien said himself would be satisfied if they would give up their arms, and that he would require no more, and requested of me to carry this message to them. Wishing to prevent bloodshed for the present, as well as greater calamities, which would inevitably follow from such a beginning, I undertook, with great danger, to ride up to the house, and to tell the police the designs of the other party. This was afterwards regarded as a lure on my part to draw the police into the views of Mr. O'Brien, and bring them over to his side. I know it was very easy to put this construction on it; but, however probable it may seem, I can say now with truth, after so many years, that I never entertained such a thought, and that, so far was I from entering into the views of the insurgent party, I wished to take no part whatever with them, and had nothing else in view but to prevent the loss of more lives, and bring matters, for that day at least, to a bloodless termination.

When I was entering the wicket in front of the house, one man, John Walsh, was lying outside the gate on his back, quite dead;* another young man named Bride, a widow's son, was dying outside the wall, having received his death wound from a bullet in passing over it. I remained with him to administer sacraments to him, and never knew any one more resigned. Walsh, indeed, had a gun when he was killed, running across the gate, the ball having passed through his lungs; but Bride had no connexion with the insurgents, but left his work that morning, and joined the crowd who followed the police, more as a looker-on than as a rebel. From the upper or lobby window the sub-inspector talked a great deal to me of the revenge that would be taken of the country for this resistance given to *himself*; that martial law would be proclaimed, houses levelled with the ground or burned, and great numbers put to death, which indeed was all probable enough: but threats of this kind did not come so well from him in his present circumstances.

Having returned to the road and stated to Mr. O'Brien and others the state of things at the house—that there were two killed, *i.e.* one dead and another dying—the people were greatly incensed, as there was no intention on their part to attack the police at the time when they wantonly and without provocation fired upon

---

* See Note 8, page 108.

them. All were anxious to return, and again Mr. O'Brien asked my advice, which was the same as before, to give up that notion and postpone hostilities to some future time. No one could appear more calm or recollected. He at once assented to my desire of not proceeding farther at present, but being taken aside and differently advised by other officers who surrounded him, he seemed disposed to listen to them. While these things were under deliberation, the Rev. Mr. Maher and I left them, with the intention, however, of returning to the place again during the evening; but after little more than two hours' absence we found that all was over without farther injury—that the police were liberated from the house, and the people dispersed. We found that reinforcements had arrived, and that the military also were coming in from every side; so that this great rebellion, so formidable and so much talked of for years, seemed at one blow to have been utterly and for ever extinguished. As Carroll, the head-constable, had gone up to the house, I waited before going up till he returned to the road. He had great difficulty, he said, in getting to the house, as they did not recognise him, and it was not till he had got over the wall surrounding it that the police recognised him, and permitted him to deliver his message. And yet, great as was his danger from the police, it was greater still at the road, when some of Mr. O'Brien's friends, Stephens especially, looking upon him as a spy, said that his message was only a pretext to execute some perfidious design. One in particular would have shot him if I had not used every exertion to protect him. After some time he was allowed to get away unhurt, of which I was very glad, as I believed him to be a very honest fellow, and that the account he gave of his mission was correct; in which opinion I was afterwards confirmed by his subsequent conduct, as well as by his impartial evidence on the trials.

I did not see the Cashel Constabulary coming in, being absent at the time, who were shortly afterwards joined by those from Thurles, under Sub-Inspector Bracken. Those from Cashel, under Sub-Inspector Cox, were the first to arrive, and made their way to the house through dense masses of people, not, indeed, without some risk, and much firing on both sides, but happily without effect. These fought much better than their pre-decessors, whom they delivered from their confinement and the imminent danger in which they were placed.

CHAPTER VIII.

CONCLUSION

I might here conclude my narrative of the Rebellion of 1848, if it deserves the name. Not unlike the mountain in labour, it resulted in nothing worthy of record, unless in exciting the fears of the government, and keeping the kingdom for so long a time in a constant state of alarm. Formidable in its progress and feeble in its execution, whilst confined to words, it was bold, menacing, and defiant; but in action, timid, irresolute, and contemptible. It is worthy of remark that the last insurrection, forty-five years before, happened also on the same day, the 23rd of July, and both were in many respects similar. Like this, the former threatened much and effected little. Its followers were numerous and enthusiastic, but unprepared and disunited. *That* was unstained by blood, except in the case of Lord Kilwarden, a good and inoffensive nobleman, whose barbarous and unprovoked assassination in the streets of Dublin was committed by the misguided adherents of Emmet, without his knowledge or concurrence. In *this* two lives were sacrificed, without any sufficient cause or necessity—a loss indeed, great in inself, and much to be regretted, but comparatively small, if we take into account the magnitude of the evil, and the manifold calamities with which we were threatened. Both were suppressed with little difficulty, and the leaders forfeited their lives to the laws of the country. One suffered the punishment of high treason on the scaffold, and expressed as his last wish that his epitaph would not be written till other times and other men would do justice to his memory, which still remains enshrined in the hearts of his countrymen. The other, after having suffered much from incarceration and exile, has been permitted at length to return to his native land, and to spend the rest of his days in the bosom of his family, and in the enjoyment of affluence and peace, and of what, I am sure, he appreciates more, in the love and affections of the people. Few will applaud their conduct or suspect their sincerity. Both loved Ireland, not wisely, but too well. Their best friends would advise them against the course they pursued, if advice could avail; and their greatest enemies never attributed to them unworthy motives. Their disinterested earnestness and ardent zeal in the cause to which they were committed, and the perils to which they exposed themselves against such fearful odds, afforded the strongest proofs of their honesty, which, in a great degree, compensated for errors of judgment.

> "—Utcunque ferent ea facta minores
> Vincet amor patriæ."

Though I had at first regretted the necessity that compelled me to be present at Farrenrory, I had reason afterwards to congratulate myself on it, and believe it to have been rather a fortunate circumstance; for, if I had not been there, it was not likely to have ended so soon. If the house were pulled down or entered forcibly, and the police killed, it would be but the commencement of hostilities. The country was arming on every side, and preparations being made everywhere throughout the kingdom to an extent hardly ever known before. The people were only waiting for a signal, and a contest of any kind would be the surest that could be given. The insurgents would receive vast accessions if there were only a delay of two or three days, and the red flame of rebellion would have blazed in every direction, and would take much more time before it could be extinguished, but at the outset it was easily suppressed, and much mischief and bloodshed at once and for ever prevented. Though the contest would in all probability be protracted and bloody, yet I did not think that, to any rational being, the issue could appear doubtful. England was at peace with the world, and from all parts of her vast and wide-spread dominions, could, without any apprehension of danger to her territorial possessions, have collected her armies together, and poured them into the country. Against such overwhelming forces, what were their resources? On the one hand, a numerous army, well appointed and disciplined, and supplied with all the munitions of war; and on the other, an undisciplined and unarmed peasantry, without leaders of any knowledge or experience in military affairs, and destitute of everything that could render success certain or even probable. This weighed also heavily with me, and was, I must confess, another reason why I wished to oppose their further progress; for that there would be carnage at all, was much to be lamented, but that it should be entirely on one side, and especially on the side of a poor and oppressed population, with whom all my sympathies were enlisted, and with whom I was in every way identified, was an idea from which I recoiled instinctively. For arms, there were a few rusty muskets in the hands of men who never carried arms before; for a *commissariat*, there were not provisions for one day; and multitudes who wished to be amongst them were prevented chiefly on this account. For general officers they had orators, men who could talk well and fight badly.* Both qualities, indeed, are seldom united in the same person. There have been some, however, who shone equally in the forum and in the camp—such was Argyle—

> "The state's whole thunder born to wield,
> And shake alike the senate and the field."

Such also was Caius Cæsar, of whom it was said, that his talents for war and eloquence were the same— "Eodem animo dixisse quo bellavit, apparuit." The Young Ireland leaders were not of this stamp. They had no superior in the cabinet, nor an inferior in the field. Some of them excelled in poetry and eloquence; others were distinguished by a clear and popular style of writing; but amongst the entire body there was not one who understood anything of the art of war. In this respect all were sadly deficient, and may have taken lessons from a school-boy or a peasant.†

---

* See Note 4, page 105.
† See Note 6, page 106.

CHAPTER IX.

ITS EFFECTS ON THE COUNTRY

Of the many bad effects of this abortive attempt at insurrection, not the least calamitous was, that by it the *prestige* of popular power seemed to have been completely annihilated. All political parties were broken up and dispersed; the public voice was silenced; and if, in the general confusion which followed, a few rational and well disposed persons still entertained better hopes of the future prosperity of Ireland, their unaided efforts could be of no avail. A few years after, in 1851, when, on the occasion of the Ecclesiastical Titles Bill, an attempt was made to bring together the broken up fragments of parties, and to adopt some plan of combined action against civil and religious persecution, the seeds of weakness and discord, sown in '48, continued still to operate, and soon dissolved this imposing and apparently powerful combination; and to this day, its grave and solemn resolutions, which, were then regarded as the foreshadowings of much future good, have been permitted to remain a dead letter.

O'Connell used to say, that any effort made by the people to redress injuries or recover their rights by force, would have the effect of throwing the country backward by half a century; and the sequel, which, happily for himself, he did not live to see, proved that never were uttered words more prophetic. This he derived from his own experience and knowledge of the former rebellion—his recollection of the massacres, confiscation, and bloodshed which followed it; and no doubt the same cycle of events was just about to begin after half a century, if, by the favourable interposition of Divine Providence, their further progress had not been arrested. With this difference, the results were no less disastrous now than formerly. The people escaped the terrible effects of martial law; they did not experience the free quarters or torture or pitch-caps or half-hangings of '98; but their political degradation could not be more complete. The exclamation of the proud Gaul to the vanquished Romans, *væ victis*, may have been inscribed on the national flag. Fallen and subdued, not from her own weakness or want of resources, but by the rash counsels and imprudence of her children, who were most anxious for her prosperity, she lay prostrate and bleeding at the feet of a foreign minister.

On the occasion of this sudden termination of hostilities, a base cry was raised by a large portion of the press of both kingdoms, vilifying the national character, and casting aspersions on it, as if Irishmen were incapable of anything chivalrous or noble; that after great threats they were able to effect nothing; that for years previous, the valour of Irishmen was the theme of every tongue; their feats at home and abroad, were subjects of declamation with writers of every class; that hitherto they had achieved victories for others, henceforward they would do so for themselves; that in future, the trophies of their warfare would not be *for* England, but *against* her, and that they burned with a desire of measuring swords with their oppessors, and wreaking on them the wrongs of seven hundred years. That such, at least in substance, was their boastful language, frequently made use of; and yet, when an opportunity was offered to them of proving their courage, they refused to accept it; that their leaders were dispersed at the approach of a few soldiers, without waiting till they came in sight; and that the whole contest, so much magnified by words, was decided in one day within the precincts of a cabbage garden.

These taunts were expressed with as much exultation as if the entire force of the kingdom were engaged in a contest with a few British troops, and completely discomfited. And yet it is certain that from the beginning the nation at large took no part in the insurrection, nor manifested any sympathy with it. Some young men of impulsive feeling and ardent patriotism, and a few of more mature age, were found, who, from every class of society, rushed inconsiderately into it; who, whilst they got credit for upright and honest motives, were looked upon by every sensible person as wild enthusiasts, who, though never dreaming of it themselves, nor intending any harm, were generally regarded by every man of sense as the greatest enemies of the country, and taking the most efficacious means to accomplish its ruin. The parish priests were nearly to a man averse to the movement, and laboured with all their might to preserve their flocks from its contagion. The senior clergy of every class, with few exceptions, abhorred it. Most of them had heard from their fathers, and some were old enough to remember, the calamitous effects of the last rebellion; but many of the younger clergy, whose want of experience was seconded by misdirected zeal, threw themselves without much reflection into its ranks, and were carried away by the example of the men who originated, but had no means of executing, this abortive scheme.

It was not, therefore, *a victory* over the nation against which the nation protested. It was rather the usual gasconade of the British and Anti-Irish press, or the growl of the Orange tiger, disappointed of his prey, having a more than usual thirst for blood, which he was not permitted to satify.

Successive administrations may differ from one another in the mode of governing this country, according to the disposition of the viceregent, or of the party he represents; but the general policy of all is the same. Whether it be Whig or Tory, or a coalition of both, the rule of Government is almost invariably by coercion. If, at any time, the better nature of the chief governor should prevail over this system, which has sometimes, though rarely happened, he is soon recalled, and another of more congenial spirit takes his place. For many generations Ireland has hardly ever tasted the sweets of paternal rule. England, which is called her sister, more resembles a step-mother; for if she should ever murmur at harsh treatment, instead of soft words or any kindness towards her, she, like Alecto, lashes her into obedience with a whip of scorpions.

The extermination of the whole Celtic race was a

project often entertained, and sometimes attempted. This was, and is indeed still, considered by some to be the only radical cure for all her complaints. In the reign of Elizabeth, Mountjoy by the destruction of the crops and standing corn, reduced the population so much that, according to the report of a distinguished actor in the scene, he could see nothing wherever he went but dead carcasses. Cromwell entered into the same plan with still greater cruelty. Wherever he passed, blood flowed in torrents; men, women, and children were slaughtered indiscriminately. Neither age, nor sex, nor helpless infancy was spared. Priests and virgins consecrated to God were butchered in crowds without mercy, and of the remnant of the people, he carried off large numbers, to colonize the islands of the West Indies.

But these efforts were in vain. The tide of population still flowed onward, and still regained its former level, or exceeded it; for, like the Israelites in Egypt, they increased the more, the more they were oppressed. Since his time there was no other attempt to effect this by violent means. Such atrocities were repugnant to the spirit of the age, especially the beginning of the last century, which has been justly regarded as the Augustan age of England. But the slow and silent operation of the penal code continued without relaxation till the reign of George III., when the sound of American arms threatened England with the loss of her colonies, and whispered to her that conciliation might be better suited to her present exigencies than coercion.

Afterwards, when the fury of the French Revolution levelled to the ground the barriers of ancient kingdoms, and threatened Europe with that deluge of blood with which it was afterwards inundated, other concessions followed; and, last of all, the greatest—the Relief-Bill—wrung from the fears of England by the indomitable energy and perseverance of one man.

During the violent struggle that preceded Catholic Emancipation, and immediately after it had been obtained, it was regarded as a final measure, which, besides the admission of Catholics to Parliament, would for ever abolish all civil and religious distinctions, and give to all the subjects of the crown an equal share in the honours and privileges of the constitution. The joy of the nation knew no bounds; but it was only short-lived. After a little experience, it was found that the same bigotry which withheld it so long, was yet able to frustrate the effect of the law, and render it a dead letter.

Writers at home and abroad extol the British constitution as the most perfect form of government, containing in itself all the others—viz., democracy, aristocracy, and monarchy. As far as regards the principles of Government, I believe this is the more general opinion, if these different parts bear a just proportion to one another; but I am sure that very few entertain any doubt that the aristocratic element, notwithstanding the more extended basis of the Reform Bill of 1832, still preponderates excessively. But with the theory of government, and the true adjustment of its parts, I have no concern. This I leave to constitutional writers, and only consider its practical effects. For I believe with Pope that, whatever be the form, "that which is best administered is best."

In Ireland especially, where the great bulk of the population is the poorest in the world, and entirely dependent on the rich, the overwhelming influence of the aristocracy absorbs everything—the making of laws and the execution of them; the appointment to all places of trust and emolument; a power which, it is unnecessary to say, is exercised to the fullest extent in behalf of their own minions, and to the exclusion of all who may entertain any sympathy for the religion or well-being of the people.

Yet all this is as nothing, compared with their power as landlords, which is the most absolute and uncontrolled that ever existed in ancient or modern times—greater than any exercised by the Janizaries of the Turkish, or the Prætorian Guards of the Roman Empire, and altogether incompatible with the spirit of a free constitution—a power of life and death, which can destroy or save, subversive alike of order, and justice, and all good government, which must be necessarily based on the protection and safety of society. By this all the other powers of the state are put in abeyance; and not only does it usurp the functions of the rest, but it makes them subservient to its own ends. It is not responsible to any other, to either the legislature or the executive; for the laws seem made only to increase its despotism, and it can command the crown to send the army, which is raised for the defence of the Empire, to demolish the cabins of the poor, and to throw them on the world to perish.

Of landlords, I speak generally and as a body; not as if there were not many honourable exceptions amongst them, most kind and benevolent to their tenants, and who feel persuaded that they have duties to fulfil as well as rights to enforce. Of this I have the testimony of my own experience, for I live under a good landlord; and in this neighbourhood, with which I have been conversant for many years, there are others equally good, some indifferently so, and none very bad; but they are such despite of laws which would degrade and corrupt them, and extinguish in their hearts every sentiment of humanity.

"Woe to those who make bad laws, and when they write, write injustice."

It may be said that from such cruelty the poor will find refuge and support in the workhouse. This, indeed, is the saddest portion of their history; for nothing else has so much contributed to complete their misery and destruction as this law, which was enacted ostensibly for their relief. It is framed especially to favour the designs of the landlord against them. And, indeed, if they required any other help besides the power with which they are already invested, for the utter extermination of the people, none could be found better suited to their purpose. One half of the board consists generally of *ex-officio* guardians, With their numerous votes by proxy, and in the double capacity of landowners and occupiers, they are also able to return a large number of the elected guardians; so that the entire board is, generally speaking, under their control. And as the poor know this very well from sad experience, the highways are crowded with them, where they would rather perish than enter the workhouse, which they look upon not a place of refuge, but as a prison of death.

This law has been a greater scourge to the country than any other that ever afflicted it, either of war, or pestilence, or famine, for it has swept the poor almost entirely away. They are gone, or as the *Times* would say, "gone with a vengeance;" and what the persecutions of Elizabeth, or the sword of Cromwell, or the dreadful ravages of a long-continued famine, could not effect, the poor law has at length accomplished.

But though the present aspect of our affairs is gloomy and discouraging, I still hope, as I have always done, that a glorious destiny awaits our unhappy country; that she will yet shake from her neck the iron yoke of the oppressor, and take her place amongst the nations of the earth. This is my belief, for I know that the iniquity of man cannot always prevail against the justice of God, whose providential care watches equally over the rich and poor, over the oppressor and the oppressed, and that in due time He will give to both the just recompense of their merit.

> "Thou art not conquered; beauty's ensign yet
> Is crimson in thy lips and in thy cheeks,
> And death's pale flag is not advanced there."

FATHER O'CARROLL'S MS.

CHAPTER X.

Father O'Carroll speaks for himself and his Parish Priest, the Rev. John Mackey

2nd Aug.—We reached home at half-past eight o'clock this evening. The Messrs. Meagher, Leyne, Cantwell, O'Donoghue, and MacManus, dined and slept in this parish last night. They are endeavouring to raise the people in different localities, but have not been successful here. They have gone up the mountains of Kilnemaugh, with the intention of mustering the people on Keeper-hill, and making a demonstration there—a hopeless mission! The country is not prepared for a rising at present,* and the clergy are hostile to such a movement. These fine disinterested young fellows are doomed men! I pity them from my heart.

4th Aug.—After dinner, at six, the P.P. and myself drove up to Parke, where we learned that the insurgent chiefs were forming the nucleus of a revolutionary party. We were introduced to them in an open field. It consisted of four persons, Messrs. Meagher, Leyne, O'Donoghue, and Cantwell. The P.P. endeavoured to dissuade them from persevering any longer in the hopeless struggle, and recommended them to fly from the country alto-

---

* See Note 7, page 107.

gether. Mr. Meagher declared he would never abandon his friends, but remain in the country to share their fate; he could, he said, easily effect his escape as many facilities were already afforded him for that purpose, but he scorned to preserve his life at the sacrifice of his honour. We endeavoured to impress on them the guilt of shedding blood, when it was clear no national good could result from it. "I had been led to believe," said Mr. Meagher, "that the nation was prepared for totally dissociating itself from England. I and my friends have made the experiment: we have found that the people are not up to the mark, and from this day forward we consider that the death of one man in our defence would be wilful murder, and for that very reason we carry no arms about us." Mr. Mackey offered to go up to Dublin to intercede with the Government in their behalf, but he would not listen to any such proposition. O'Donoghue, certainly the most determined and warlike looking man amongst them, was of opinion that they ought to be allowed to leave the country, but the others overruled him. They resolved on taking different directions for the night. O'D. said he did not know a mortal in the entire province, whilst the other gentleman had friends in different parts of the country, who would shelter and protect them. We left them at ten, without being able to effect the object of our mission.

6th Aug.—I went at the request of the P.P. to see the outlaws, who, I heard, were concealed in a house near Cloneyharp. As I reached the place they had just taken to flight in different directions, as a courier came in to announce to them that two troops of dragoons were approaching to capture them. They passed on however in the direction of Tipperary. It had rained very heavily for the last half-hour, and when I afterwards met them in the fields, they were completely drenched with wet. One's heart would have melted at the sight. Mr. Leyne said in a whisper to Mr. Meagher that they should procure something to eat. I observed that they must be sadly in need of some refreshment, and that if they came with me, I had no doubt but Mr. Mackey would feel happy to give them a dinner at his house. Mr. Leyne embraced the proposition, but Mr. M. said he would not expose him to danger by entering his house. I then proposed to serve them with some refreshment in the fields, on the rere of the house. To this all parties agreed, I came away to apprize Mr. Mackey of what had taken place. Anne would not consent to have dinner served to them in the fields, but required they should dine with ourselves. Poor fellows, they made a bad dinner, though they did not taste a morsal [sic] of animal food for several days before.

It was agreed during the evening that Mr. Mackey should start for Dublin on to-morrow to propose to the Government terms on which they were prepared to surrender. His instructions were to this effect: "Mr. Meagher and his friends will surrender themselves to the Government, on condition that they and all others concerned in the late outbreak be permitted to leave the country altogether." I doubt much if the Government will accede to these terms. I do not think that any English Government in this country is capable of acting in a generous and forgiving spirit. No matter. It is good to make the experiment. Anne has influenced Mr. Mackey to entertain them for this night. He consented, and they have now retired to rest. The servants are keeping watch in the fields and avenues leading to the house.

Anne remained up all night apprehending a visit from the police. I retired to bed at half-past three o'clock, after having visited the outposts. Mr. Mackey left for Dublin a little after six, to lay his propositions before the Government. Our visitors were ready for breakfast at eleven, and entertained themselves in the garden up to dinner hour. After dinner, Anne, myself, and the servants held a council, as to whether there would be danger of arrest, if we entertained them this night also. Anne was of opinion that we should hazard every danger sooner than unhouse them. It was finally agreed on without dissent that they should sleep here to-night. After tea, Mr. Leyne sang the "Memory of the Dead." He has a fine rich voice. All parties retired to rest at eleven in good spirits. After visiting the watches I went to bed at half-past two o'clock.

8th Aug.—Breakfast at ten. I had a sick call to Ruane, and made enquiries of several persons if they had any knowledge where the outlaws were concealed, and was told they were traced to our neighbourhood on Sunday evening; but that the prevailing opinion now is, that they proceeded in the direction of Tipperary, where one of them was arrested. I was glad to find that no suspicion rested on our house, especially as the country is full of spies and detectives. Dinner as usual at five. It was thought prudent to remove them for this night. Beds were procured for them at Mr. Edward B's. I went over at eleven in the darkness of the night, and after seeing them comfortably lodged, returned and wrote to Mrs. O'C., of Ennis, at the request of Mr. Leyne.

9th Aug.—Went over for the visitors to bring them to breakfast, but having been asked to breakfast where they slept—they did so. I had two sick calls. Very heavy showers detained me on the way, and having returned found our visitors amusing themselves in the garden. After dinner sent one of the servants to Pat Keeffe's, who lives in a very retired and solitary spot, to request he would provide beds for our friends for one night. Having made many protestations of friendship, he and his wife refused to do so. After many suggestions, it is at length resolved that they should remain here for this night. The reason of our desire to have them removed occasionally to some less frequented place, arises from the danger of discovery, so many persons coming here on business. On this day a letter was received from Mr. Mackey less encouraging than one received on yesterday. Mr. Under-Secretary Reddington made great promises at the first interview, and that he would procure a private audience for him with the Lord Lieutenant. The following day he was quite reserved in his manner, and retracted all the professions made the day before.

FATHER O'CARROLL'S MS.

10th Aug.—All our friends here still. Mr. Hogan ran in breathless haste to say that he saw two dragoons approaching the house. Our visitors jumped through the parlour window into the garden, with the intention of taking to the mountains, but after a little time the dragoons went on to Thurles.

11th Aug.—We got the *Evening Mail* to-day with our own papers. The whole business has got out, and the *Mail* has completely distorted the object of Mr. Mackey's mission. It represents him as sent by the insurgents to beg their lives of the government—an atrocious falsehood! Mr. Meagher and his friends begged of me in the most passionate manner to write to Mr. Mackey forthwith to contradict that statement, and set them right before the public. I wrote a letter to Mr. Mackey, which had the approbation of the entire party. Before it was despatched, I offered my services in any way I could be of use to them, and to go up to Dublin to impress on Mr. M. the instant necessity of contradicting so base a calumny. My proposition was adopted, and accordingly I started at three for Thurles—dined there, and left on the half-past five train for Dublin. Saw Mr. Mackey, who had the whole misstatement of the *Mail* contradicted in the evening papers of the next day.

12th Aug.—Left Dublin this morning on the eleven o'clock train—in Thurles at three, and reached Clonoulty at eight. Saw the gentlemen, and communicated to them the result of my mission. I then explained to them the danger they were in of being arrested, and impressed on them the necessity of adopting some decided course, but found them still as undetermined as ever. They would neither surrender, nor endeavour to escape. I left them at ten, somewhat annoyed at their want of decision. Three policemen were stationed outside the chapel all day in care of a proclamation, posted on the chapel gate, offering £300 reward for the arrest of Richard O'Gorman. Mr. Cantwell left his friends last night, intending to make his escape.

13th Aug.—I had the last mass at Clonoulty. On my way to the chapel learned from a policeman that Messrs. Meagher, Leyne, and O'Donoghue were arrested a little beyond the police barrack at Rathkennan, on their way to Thurles, about one o'clock this morning—sad news! It appears they left about eleven last night, with the intention of going to Cashel, and not knowing the country went in the direction of Thurles. After passing the police-station of Rathkennan, without attracting any notice, Leyne stopped behind to light his cigar. A police patrol under constable Madden came up with Meagher and O'Donoghue in the meantime without a challenge, Meagher having completely thrown them off their guard by the nonchalance and good humour with which he bade them "good night." On meeting Leyne, who was just coming out from a peasant's hut as they passed, they challenged him, and having demanded of him to tell them whither he was going, he answered, "to Cashel." They instantly arrested him, and pursued his companions, whom they also arrested without resistance.

FATHER O'CARROLL'S MS.

I will now remark that whilst our visitors were here I took down the heads of the various transactions connected with the late unhappy outbreak. The organization was more extensive than most persons think. Had the leaders got time to mature all their plans, there is no doubt but the movement would have been formidable. The suspension of the Habeas Corpus Act precipitated the crisis, and the clubs were taken completely by surprise. These said clubs, after a great deal of bravado, showed the white feather, when called on to give effect to their professions; and I do not at all feel disappointed in my estimate of them. They expected that a few half-famished and unarmed peasants in Tipperary ought to effect a revolution for them. Nor is my opinion of the principal leaders much higher. With a few exceptions, they are men totally incapable of conducting such a movement to a successful issue, though they had at their command all the elements of success. I never heard of so many instances of incapacity in any one pretending to be a leader as in S. O'Brien. If a country were to be revolutionized solely from the rostrum or editor's desk they would have been powerful agents, but they were entirely unfitted for the drudgery of a camp, or the toil and fatigue of a campaign. Besides they had no reason to believe that the great mass of the population sympathized with them. The result has proved that they were regarded with suspicion or indifference. Dillon and MacManus, with perhaps, Leyne and O'Gorman, were, in this respect, the best qualified amongst them.

22nd Aug.—Received at Templemore a package of letters, in which there was one from Mr. Leyne, requesting an interview with me in Kilmainham prison, in case I should come to Dublin. He desires to procure some religious books, and to perform a spiritual retreat during his imprisonment.

23rd Aug.—Met Miss P., who accompanied me to the Castle, and wrote a note to Under Secretary Reddington, requesting permission to see Mr. Leyne, but he refused making an order for that purpose, till Mr. L. intimated to him in writing a desire to see me. I could not, however, wait in Dublin to see him, but Miss P. … engaged to have a letter from him on my return from the Isle of Man.

2nd Sept.—Returned from the Isle of Man and saw Miss P., who accompanied me to the Castle. and got an order from the U. S. to visit Mr. Leyne at Kilmainham on Monday next.

4th—Saw Mr. L. and O'Donoghue, who told me they regretted not having taken my advice, and endeavoured to escape.

11th—This evening I had a letter from Mr. Leyne, requesting me to go to see him in Clonmel.

12th—Started at nine o'clock this morning for Cashel, and thence, at half-past one o'clock, for Clonmel, where I arrived at half-past three, and saw Mr. Meagher at six.

13th—Got an order from the High Sheriff to visit the state prisoners in the jail; spent an hour or two with them, and was introduced to Mr. MacManus after his return from the Court-house, whither he had been conveyed during the morning to hear his sentence. He appeared in very good spirits, and spoke with freedom and animation of the scenes through which he had lately passed. He is a fine handsome young fellow, full of soul and longing to have another opportunity of doing some service for his country. Had the other leaders possessed the same energy of mind and acted on his suggestions, the movement would have been more general and formidable, and would not have terminated so contemptibly.

He appeared delighted at seeing me, and met me with the cordiality of an old friend. He requested of me to accept from him a small dressing case, as a slight memorial of his esteem and respect for me. His fellow-prisoners must have been speaking of me to him, otherwise I could not expect to have so much of his confidence and regard. I spent nearly an hour with him and his relative, the Rev. Mr. Tierney, P. P., of Clontibert, who had been one of the State Prisoners in '44. Saw poor O'Donoghue in the dock, and spoke a few words to him. He asked me to stop in town and hear his confession, as, said he, I am a great sinner this time past. I told him I could not, as being of another diocese, and not having faculties in the diocese of Waterford, but that I would procure a Clergyman for him. He at once assented. He said his trial was a mere farce, and wished it at an end, and I own though inclined to offer some words of hope, I could not so belie my own conviction as to express one word of encouragement. The jury is what is usually in Tipperary called a "hanging jury," and it is vain to entertain the remotest hope of even a disagreement.

Leyne is not to be tried, which, I assured him, I believed a fortunate circumstance, for though no positive evidence of complicity could be brought against him, the fact of his being arrested in the company of Meagher and O'Donoghue would be enough for a Tipperary jury to bring in a verdict of "Guilty." Mr. M. is bearing up with his usual fortitude, and is the general favorite. I advised him to prepare himself as a Christian for his impending fate. He assured me he was thinking seriously on the subject, and that he considered he had done a good part of the business already, as he had made a confession of his whole life before embarking in the fatal struggle in which all his hopes were wrecked. O'D., he says, drinks grog to keep up his spirits, and is sometimes a little wayward, and we have been thinking that you are the only person most likely to bring him to a sense of his situation, and the grave duties it enjoins. I brought a letter from Mr. M. to Anne, thanking her for himself and his friends, and for her kind attention to them whilst here. They are occupied the greater part of the day in giving their autographs to ladies, etc.

1849.

8th March—Had a sick call at Rossmore. On my return found Mr. Leyne before me. He and Mr. Mackey dine to-day at Longfield.

12th—Messrs. Leyne and Mackey went this morning

to Clonmel, at six o'clock, where the former is to remain during the assizes, and hold himself ready for trial if called on.

THOMAS F. MEAGHER TO MISS MACKEY.

Clonmel Jail, October 18th, 1848.

My dear Miss Mackey,

I should have to accuse myself of great unkindliness and ingratitude, did I not avail myself of Father O'Carroll's visit to convey to you my warm and sincere thanks, for the anxious care you bestowed upon me when I was an outcast in the land of my birth, my love and my ambition.

Indeed I ought to have done so long since, but perhaps these thanks are all the kindlier for having been deferred till now, and may prove to you that I have retained from the first to the last day of my imprisonment, a lively recollection of your sympathy and attention.

In these sentiments my friends, Mr. Leyne and Mr. O'Donoghue, most warmly concur, and as a slight testimony of their truth, we beg your acceptance of the accompanying book, the only one we can procure in time for Father O'Carroll's departure.

I know you will not judge of our feelings from the poverty of the present, many a plain coarse stone in our old green church-yards commemorates more virtue than the gilded costly effigies that crowd the Cathedral aisles of rich and noble cities; and there is more heart, God knows, in these poor church-yards, on funeral days, than

ever throbbed in the glittering wake of kings and princes.
With sincere esteem and gratitude,
Believe me, my dear Miss Mackey,
Yours most faithfully,.
THOMAS FRANCIS MEAGHER.

And this generous and noble-hearted woman richly
merited the praise of Mr. Meagher and his fellow-prisoners, for when her brother, the late lamented P.P. and
his most estimable curate (since alas! numbered with
the dead,) refused to admit them into the house, she
overcame the fears of both, and would not allow dinner
to be served to them in the fields, but had them brought
in and seated at her own table; and when they were exposed to the danger of death from cold and famine, was
to them a ministering angel, solicitous for their wants,
and watchful for their safety.

NOTES

(*Note* 1)

Mr. Dillon escaped in a sailing vessel, from the western coast, bound for America, disguised as a Priest. The captain, who was glad to have a clergyman on board, invited him to the cabin and to his own table. No person knew him save one—this was P. J. Smith—who had been a Confederate himself, and was now in the same danger as Mr. Dillon. When they had reached about midway a couple amongst the passengers wished to be united in marriage, and hoped his reverence would kindly perform the ceremony. He was perplexed for some time, but soon contrived to extricate himself from his difficult position. After a minute inquiry, he found the parties could not be married without a dispensation from the Bishop, and that it was therefore necessary to postpone the ceremony till they would have landed in America.

(*Note* 2)

This was to be the central meeting-place, from whence they were to proceed to Kilkenny, seize on the cattle at the show, and make the Lord Lieutenant and the Dukes of Cambridge and Leinster prisoners, and retain them as hostages.

(*Note* 3)

The circumstances attending the first meeting of O'Donoghue and Stephens are so peculiar that I consider them deserving of notice. As soon as O'Donoghue heard that S. O'Brien had raised the standard of revolt in Tipperary, he paid a visit to Newgate to Gavan Duffy, who gave him a letter for S. O'Brien, to be delivered to him with his own hand. He started for Kilkenny, and arrived there late on Monday evening. He was entirely a stranger in the town, and sought information from the waiter of the hotel, telling him at the same time that he had a letter for Mr. O'Brien, which it was important he should deliver quickly. The waiter thinking he was a detective, went out on some pretext, and ran to the club-room to communicate his suspicions to the members. It being late, all had left except Stephens and another—a town councillor. Stephens desired him to return and keep him in conversation for some time, and that he would be with him very soon. Armed with a case of pistols, he went to the hotel, conversed with O'Donoghue for some time, and at a signal from the waiter that the coast was clear, he presented a pistol at his head, ordered him to accompany him, and to consider himself his prisoner. O'Donoghue had no alternative—a car was in readiness, on which all three mounted, viz.: Stephens, O'Donoghue, and the town councillor. Passing through Thurles O'Donoghue was recognised by P. J. Smith, who recommended him to Stephens as an honest Confederate, and no detective. On which he obtained his liberty. They reached Cashel about 10 o'clock on Tuesday, just as S. O'B. was preparing to leave for Killenaule and Mullinahone. O'Donoghue delivered the letter—the celebrated letter which was afterwards abstracted from his portmanteau, and brought on the Under-Secretary so much obloquy and censure.

(*Note* 4)

I have no intention of detracting from the merits of the Leaders taken individually, I believe they were all brave men, and that there was not a recreant amongst them. Every one who volunteered to join the movement, knew the perils which he encountered, and the penalties which he incurred, and that his first stop on such a course in case of failure, was at the risk of his life. There was no lack of courage or patriotism amongst them, but as a body, they were utterly contemptible and unqualified for such an enterprise. Not one of them was acquainted with military science, nor fit to lead a regiment, much less an army into the field. It has been often said, that an army of stags headed by a lion, is more formidable than an army of lions commanded by a stag. Taken in a literal sense in the present instance, this is not appropriate as amongst the chiefs, at least there were no cowards; but, if for cowardice you substitute ignorance, or incapacity, it is perfectly so, with this difference, that it applies equally to both. The chieftains, as well as their followers, were alike unskilful, and under such Leaders, to expose a defenceless and unarmed multitude, to disciplined troops would be to commit them to indiscriminate slaughter. When I say they could fight badly, I wish to signify that they embarked in this fearful struggle, without due preparation, and neglected to compare their own resources with the forces arrayed against them; unlike the wise king spoken of in the Gospel, who, when he saw "that his enemy had twice as many men at his command, and that he was unable to contend with him, sent him an embassy of peace, and wished to be reconciled with him.

(*Note* 5)

At this time, and for many years past, Mr. Prendergast was of weak mind. He was never an ardent politician, and was now, quite indifferent concerning such matters. He loved excitement and for this, he would join either party, or both. Hearing of a great gathering at Mullinahone, he hastened thither, and having met the procession on the way, he took his place at its head. There was great joy, for though a P. P. only in name, he would have increased their influence very much with the people, had not its effect been counteracted a few hours later in the day, by Mr. O'Brien's ill-omened speech at Ballingarry. His accession to their ranks was not of long duration, for in a few days after he visited the camp at Ballingarry, and felt quite as happy with the military as with the insurgents.

(*Note* 6)

Of this the following anecdote, which I heard from a person of the same district, affords a proof. One day in his wanderings through the hills of Kilnamanagh, Mr. Meagher entered the cabin of a poor mountaineer just as they were about sitting down to dinner, such as it was, very humble indeed, yet with true Irish hospitality, no less visible in offering a portion of their poor and scanty fare, than at the costly and luxurious tables of the rich. This was prefaced by an expression of regret, that it was not better and more suitable for him, and as "hunger is good sauce," he cheerfully accepted the invitation. During the meagre repast, the apostle of revolution considered it a fitting opportunity to inveigh against the Government and their rulers, who, by bad and oppressive laws, reduced a noble peasantry to such misery. He expected, of course, a sympathetic answer, imprecations against such tyranny, with a vow to rise against it as one man, as soon as the present movement was sufficiently matured to require it. He was however disappointed, for the man of the house simply said, poor as it is we prefer it, and are content, for we know the Government will not let us starve. This answer pained Mr. Meagher exceedingly.

(*Note* 7)

PROGRAMME OF MR. MEAGHER'S IRISH REPUBLIC.

1. Whole and absolute independance [sic] of England.

2. Declaration of an Irish Republic.

3. Political equality of all creeds.

4. Confiscation of the property of all found in arms against the Irish Republic.

5. Immediate formation of a National Guard, into which the military and police were admissible.

6. Strict observance of all private and commercial contracts.

7. Contributions in money and kind to be levied on the faith of the Irish Republic.

8. Oblivion of all distinctions of race and creed.

Doheny was for taking the money from the banks of Carrick and Clonmel in case those towns were taken, and K—— was for taking hostages from the aristocracy and their abettors, and every means of sustenance.

Contemporaneously with the issue of this proclamation the green flag was to be hoisted from the tower on St. Patrick's rock. It is needless to remark, that neither was the green flag hoisted, nor the proclamation issued. Whether such an event will ever come to pass is a question, the solution of which rests with the Government, and which will depend chiefly on their wisdom or imprudence.

(*Note* 8)

Besides two killed, a great many received gun-shot wounds—amongst others, Cavanagh was disabled by a bullet received in the leg, and was taken on a litter to a neighbouring house, where he lay concealed till night, when he was removed to a more distant and safer place. Stephens was not wounded on this day, though it was otherwise reported. I met him after the firing had ceased, and he appeared as usual in his whole skin.

(*Note* 9)

In page 15 of his pamphlet, in reply to mine, Mr. Trant says, quoting these words: "It was ungrateful in Father Fitzgerald to misrepresent me, who gave him his life, which I could have legally taken." This reminds one of the fable of the fox and the stork.

And at page 4 he says: "Had I then known that Carroll was in collusion with him, I would decidedly have shot him on the spot." From which it appears that if Carroll and I escaped with our lives, on that occasion, we are less indebted to the clemency or gratitude of Mr. Trant than to the merciful interposition of Divine Providence.

APPENDIX

As the following letter may throw additional light on the subject, it is now republished, having been written by me, soon after the insurrection:—

TO THE EDITOR OF THE FREEMAN.

Ballingarry, 13th November, 1848.

Sir—As the part which I took in the affair at Farren-rory has been much misrepresented, and that, instead of a peace-maker, I have been considered a partisan, you will be so good as to allow me, through the columns of the *Freeman*, to say a few words in self-defence, especially as my motives and conduct, which, whatever be their merit, ought to be referred exclusively to myself, are by an inference as illogical as it is unjust, charged upon the whole order to which I have the unmerited honour to belong.

In the first place, with regard to my motives, I must say that they could not be partial or previously formed, as it was my fixed resolution not to interfere in this long expected "outbreak"—to look on with melancholy and painful, but silent, indifference—and not to be implicated in the movement at all, either for or against it. This determination I had come to because I detested alike Whiggery and Young Irelandism. The principles of both, however opposite, seemed to me equally pernicious, so that whichever would be vanquished, Ireland would be a gainer, and if both perished (I mean the parties, not the men) we might entertain a hope of her resurrection. And, with regard to the former, my hatred of it arose from the recollection of the misery to which the people were reduced by their misgovernment during the last two years, the sufferings which they at present endure, and the prospect of being subjected to still greater calamities during the coming winter, when they are threatened with the double scourge of pestilence and famine, without much hope of sympathy or aid from others to alleviate those evils. In the scenes through which they have passed they exhibited proofs of patient endurance to which the records of time afford no parallel—which no other nation, in similar circumstances, would submit to—and, to expect that the same systematic disregard of the lives of the people could be continued without any effort to resist it, would be to admit that we know but little of the feelings and passions of human nature and of the examples of terrible retribution to be met with at every period of the history of the world. For this reason it appeared to me that any exhortation to farther patience was quite unnecessary, as they already eminently excelled others in the practice of this virtue, even those who would undertake to instruct them.

No one could be more anxious to inculcate the observance of the laws, respect for the throne, and obedience to all legitimate authority, believing, as I do, that every power is from God, and that our obedience should be the dictate of conscience, not the result of necessity. But all legislation should be for the common good. To this fundamental law every other should be referred. *Salas populi suprema lex*. On this basis the whole fabric of society, to be permanent, should be erected; or, if built on any other, it will be agitated and wrecked by every tempest. Laws should not be made for any creed or class, but for the benefit of all, without any distinction of sect or party. Is this the character of British legislation for this country? Can it be assumed of the boasted wisdom of the imperial parliament, that it consults impartially for the general welfare of the whole state?—or, rather is not its whole spirit, in legislating on Irish subjects, to sacrifice the interists [sic] of the many to those of a few—to direct the whole current of national wealth into the coffers of landlordism—and for this purpose, in violation of the laws of nature and of God, to reduce the population to a convenient standard by extermination and famine? As such a course, therefore, seems to me to be adapted to exasperate the people, and to provoke them to rebellion, whether designed to do so or not, I formed the resolution to take no pains to suppress it, lest I may counteract the intention of our rulers, or incur their displeasure.

And, with regard to Young Irelandism, I must say that I never had any connexion or sympathy with it. I believed its leaders, for the most part, to be chivalrous, self-devoted, and sincere, but greatly mistaken. I always considered that their doctrines had a necessary tendency to civil war; and, as a minister of religion and of peace, I felt bound to discountenance them. Even prudence, and a concern for the people's lives, if I had not other and higher motives, would not allow me to encourage what I thought to be a rash and ruinous attempt at rebellion; and, in whatever light my conduct on that occasion may be viewed, either now or hereafter, to myself it will be always a subject of proud consciousness that my efforts contributed to check the progress of a movement which, without being productive of any advantage, would have deluged the country with blood.

To be convinced of this, it will be just enough to compare the condition of England at the time with ours. She had amongst us a powerful police force, augmented and organized for the anticipated outbreak—a considerable number of our population willing and ready to arm in her cause—disengaged from war elsewhere, and at peace with the world, she could concentrate against us, on the shortest notice, her undiminished resources on sea and land. To this Ireland, impoverished and famine-stricken, could only oppose an emaciated, half-starved population, bent to the earth by years of unexampled misery, unable to carry not only arms, but themselves; without a treasury, without ammunition, without *food*; destitute of all that could render them formidable, to an enemy, and possessed of everything that could make them abject and contemptible. I am not for a contest at all; but if I were, it would not be such a contest as this, in which all the chances are on one side, and none at all on the other.

England will not be always equally disembarrassed. Difficulties may yet come upon her, when Ireland, instead of receiving, may dictate terms, and entirely disclaim the legislative connection with her good sister. Such a case occurred before, and may again—it is possible at least—when she may have cause to lament the consequences of her misgovernment; for if a heavy retribution does not await her, I would be almost disposed to doubt the existence of an all-ruling Providence, or find it very difficult to reconcile a long impunity of the most gigantic crimes with the constant and immutable decrees of eternal justice.

I thought it proper to state so far my political creed, to show that I had no inclination to be numbered on that occasion with either party,—as little disposed to be a policeman as a "rebel," and only to be a mediator between both, that I may put a stop to hostilities for the present, and prevent, if possible, the effusion of blood. Whether the part I afterwards took in the transaction was in accordance with this resolution, will appear from a plain unbiassed narrative of facts.

On Saturday, the day of this occurrence, on which it is usual with the clergy to attend in their chapels, I happened to be at Ballingarry, when, between ten and eleven o'clock, a considerable body of police passed by on their way to the Commons, where Smith O'Brien had arrived the evening before. It being known that he would not allow himself to be arrested unless by force, and as it was therefore certain that a battle must ensue, I left the chapel and moved on slowly in the same direction. There were crowds along the road, as was to be expected on an occasion of so much excitement, without any intention, as far as I could discover, of being at all concerned in the affray, but observing attentively the motions of the police, as the whole line of way is visible, from the village to the Commons. The hearts of many, no doubt, throbbed with painful anxiety for the safety of a man, who without any previous acquaintance, had thrown himself unexpectedly amongst them, who, regardless of the dignity of birth and station unmindful of the ties of family and kindred, of the happiness and endearing attachment of home, preferred to take his place amongst the poorest of the people, who were told that all these sacrifices were made for them, and that he was now prepared to lay down his life in their cause. In their feelings of sympathy for him I confess that I participated largely, and though my chief object in going was to warn the people against any violation of the law, and to maintain the peace of the parish, I was resolved to do so without adding but as little as possible to the difficulties of his already perilous circumstances. At the time there was not the slightest appearance that mediation of any kind was practicable, but it occurred to me that events might take some unforseen turn to afford such an opportunity, or, if not, that my assistance might be of use to the wounded and the dying. And such an opportunity did afterwards occur, for, as the Rev. Mr. Meagher* and I were talking on the road side, a man rode up, of rather respectable appearance, who joined in our conversation, told us that he was a policeman who had a message to Mr. Trant, and that, if we went with him we might altogeth-

---

* Presumably this was intended to read 'Maher'?—*Editor.*

er—he by his influence with the police, and we with the people—be able to propose terms of peace, and stop the firing which had commenced a few minutes before, and was then kept up without intermission. Accordingly, we at once rode on with full speed, till we arrived underneath Mrs. Cormick's house, from which volleys of musketry still came forth, which compelled us to take shelter under cover of the fences, that in this place enclosed the road on both sides. Here a large crowd was assembled also for shelter, many of them greatly excited, who had just returned from the house, where one man was shot dead, and a considerable number severely wounded. I had an understanding with Carroll, the policeman, that when he arrived at the house, and would have spoken to the police, he would make a signal for me to go to him. In his first attempt to get up at the rere of the house, his danger was so great that he was compelled to return. In a second effort, however, he was more successful; he made his way up safely, and after delivering his message and communicating with Mr. Trant, he gave the signal agreed upon with me to come to him. I went up in front of the house, and, having entered the yard, inquired for the officer, who appeared immediately at the upper window, and after ascertaining who I was, and hearing that I was come to make peace, he expressed himself very thankful. He began to say that he was not the aggressor— that it was not he that commenced hostilities—that he would not have fired if he were not attacked; to which I answered, that with whatever was past I had nothing to do, that my business was only to reconcile parties for the present, and to prevent further mischief; for which he thanked me again repeatedly. He then proceeded to say that his position was a strong one—that the house was well fortified and provisioned, and that he could not be conquered unless it were burned, which, he was sure, could not be easily effected; and that they would never surrender their arms but with their lives. These things he expressed with great rapidity and vehemence. He seemed also much excited for he made use of violent gestures. All the horrors of war seemed present to his imagination, for he said that in consequence of this resistance to *himself*, houses would be levelled with the ground, towns and villages would be burned, and the country subjected to martial law. As soon as I perceived there was any chance of being heard, I said: "Mr. Trant, what would you think if I could prevail with the people and with Mr. O'Brien, whom I had not yet consulted, to allow you and your men to go away with your arms uninjured?" To which he replied, that though he felt very grateful, and though he entertained no doubt of my good disposition he considered himself more secure where he was; that he knew the influence of priests was not so great now as heretefore, and would not leave his present stronghold for any protection that I could promise him. Of course this answer rendered any further attempt at mediation on my part quite unnecessary, as he did not require it, and deemed himself more safe where he was than any exertions of mine could make him.

This is a simple statement of the conversation that I had with Mr. Trant which is so much at variance with the testimony attributed to him on the state trials as to seem almost unaccountable. It may be that he was misunderstood by the reporter, or that, in the confusion in which he seemed to be while I was speaking to him, he forgot what occurred (for I do not suspect him of any wilful misstatement;) but whatever may be the cause, certain it is that what is given in the newspapers is a tissue of falsehood from beginning to end, for the whole tenor of the published discourse makes me only a representative of the insurgent party, covertly endeavouring to get the police into their power, and as the Chief Justice expressed it, though he had evidence of the contrary, alternately making use of promises and threats to induce them to give up their arms.

It would be ungrateful, to say the least of it, in Mr. Trant to misrepresent me, who exposed my life to protect his and to prevent bloodshed;* for in all probability, he owed his life then, and does at this moment, to my interference; and the great feats which he performed on that day would be for ever lost to the world, or if told at all, they should have some other trumpeter besides the *general* himself.

As he was so thankful, and complimentary to me in my presence, when he was in the midst of danger, he ought not to criminate me in my absence, when danger was far away. For, if it had not been within the sphere of

---

* See Note 9, page 109.

my spiritual labours, where religion and humanity required my assistance, the affair at Farrenrory would have passed away without my personal knowledge—I would not be suspected of being with the police or against them, for the government or opposed to it, for I could not have been there at all. And this indifference, or, as it was called, hostility, was perfectly understood by both, for Mr. O'Brien believed that his failure was owing to the opposition of the clergy, and Mr. Trant considered us, though somewhat disguised, no better than Leaders of the insurrection. But it is always the mediator's misfortune to displease both sides, and this was exactly our case; for, throughout the state trials there seemed to be, both on the part of the crown and on the part of the defence, a premediated intention to leave us as much as possible the subjects of public odium—to give to our efforts a false direction, and to make our character to appear anything but in its true light.

Carroll, who ought to know more of the whole proceedings than any one else, being at one time linked with the crowd, and at another in conversation with the police, and who was both honest and willing enough to declare what he knew, was kept back, as if through design, and his testimony elicited with much caution and reserve; whilst Mr. Trant, who was closely shut up the whole time, and whose mind was entirely occupied with notions of his his own prowess, and the glorification of the police, was drawn out at great length and placed in full relief.* But, whatever a priest does, he is sure to be maligned. This he expects from long experience, and for this he is prepared. Yet, through good and evil report, his conduct is unchanged, uninfluenced by the censure or applause of men—he pursues the same undeviating course, guided only by a sense of duty and of the obligations he owes to God, to the people, and the throne, of which, though reviled, he is the firmest bulwark and the best support.

Yours, faithfully,

P. Fitzgerald.

---

* See Note 9, page 109.

OTHER REPRINTS PUBLISHED BY BOOKS ULSTER

Betsy Gray or Hearts of Down ~ W. G. Lyttle

ISBN 978-1910375211

The Bush that Burned ~ Lydia Foster

ISBN: 978-1910375112

Popular Rhymes and Sayings of Ireland ~ John J. Marshall

ISBN: 978-1910375037

Sayings, Proverbs and Humour of Ulster ~ Sir John Byers

ISBN: 978-0954306380